Table of Contents

Why Me? Why This Book?

I'll never forget the night that inspired me to write this book. It's not a happy story, but it will hopefully make my motives and intentions very clear. I was working the late shift in the ER when I noticed a young woman with a towel over her face being escorted into a treatment room. When I went in to introduce myself and begin my examination, I noted a black, swollen eye with a large bleeding wound just above it.

Despite the fact that she was crying, I could immediately tell by the warm and friendly way she greeted me that she was very nice and had an engaging personality.

"What happened?" I asked.

"I fell down the stairs," she replied, tears running down her face, her eyes fixed firmly on the linoleum tiled floor.

As I sat down to begin repairing her wound, I said, "How did this really happen?"

The truth was that she had gotten into a fight with her boyfriend, who had "accidentally" hit her in the face with the heel of her shoe. Since it was a quiet night in the ER, I was able to sit there listening to her for over an hour as I sutured her laceration.

What bothered me the most about what she said is that I wasn't surprised by any of it. That's how much her story had in common with what I've heard from so many other women having trouble in their relationships. The same insecurities. The same self-defeating questions: "Why do I feel so unhappy?" "Why am I so in love with him?" "He tells me that he loves me, so why does he rarely act like it?" "Doesn't he realize that I'd do anything for him?"

That young woman had completely lost herself and her sense of confidence. And the end result was an extreme consequence of what those losses can lead to. I remember feeling frustrated. Frustrated that she would stay with this man. Frustrated that so many women seem clueless when it comes to happiness in relationships. She had become an insecure, desperate, unhappy woman who was completely dependent on a man (if you want to call him that) for her self-worth.

If any of those feelings sound familiar, you're in good company. Putting up with a violent temper is only the most dangerous example of the many ways in which women sell themselves short in their relationships. If you're anything like the women I know, you may not have been physically abused in the past, but you have probably settled for a lot less attention, appreciation, respect, and consideration than you are worth. Every time you take a call from a guy you'd sworn off because he didn't return the messages you left him two weeks ago, or accept a guy back after he cheated on you, or even so much as wordlessly let him yammer away on his cell phone during your dinner date, you've allowed yourself to settle for a whole lot less than you deserve.

As an ER doctor, I am in a unique position. I often see people at their weakest moments. I have seen the devastation on a woman's face when she realizes the hard way that she has lost her sense of self—more times than I want to remember. I would like to offer you the kind of advice that will hopefully prevent you from ever feeling anywhere near as helpless and unhappy as the young woman I described earlier. You deserve better from yourself and you deserve better from the men in your life.

Don't Be That *Girl*

If you ask me, any book called *Don't Be That Girl* had better not be *that* book. So here's what I'm not going to do: I'm not going to sit here and try to tell you how to please a man. I'm not going to drone on and on about the differences between men and women. And I'm definitely not going to claim to know what he is thinking, why he didn't call back, or what in the world he may have meant when he said, "I think you're great."

Let's leave the armchair psychology to the amateurs, because happy people, be they single or otherwise, know that successful dating is all about *you*. In this book, I am going to create a new cliché: Don't be *that* girl or you'll end up with *that* guy.

Let me start by saying that there are plenty of great guys out there. Before you waste another day driving yourself crazy, trying to analyze what in the world is wrong with him—and what you can do to change him—I am going to let you in on a little secret: It may not be him. It may be you. He may not be a jerk. And he's not necessarily afraid of commitment. He may only be afraid of a commitment with *you*. Why? Because what he is fearful of—and I have to say, often rightly so—is that you might be *that* girl.

Need specifics? Well, here are some of the red flags that tip us guys off to the possibility that, yikes, we may be dating *that* girl:

- She's the one with an agenda. She already pictures the white picket fence after two dates and she'll do anything to make sure her "plan" materializes.
- She's the agreeable one who will go along with his every wish. When she's dating a football fanatic, she's dressing in his team's jerseys and painting her face in his team's colors. When she moves on to the wannabe rock star, she's hanging out at band practice and channeling Pamela Anderson.
- She's the drama queen who becomes overly emotional anytime a guy breathes incorrectly.
- She's the miserable, angry one who makes sure that she spreads her bad energy wherever she goes.
- She's the insecure girl who is uncomfortable in her own skin and is never certain if she's good enough for him.
- She's the girl who will suddenly turn into a completely different person the minute a guy enters the room.
- She's the desperate one who truly believes that if she lets this one get away, then it's all over. She'll do anything to keep him. (And in the process, she'll unwittingly do everything possible to push him away!)
- She's the career-obsessed woman who claims not to have time for a relationship.
- She's the one who constantly finds herself stuck in an unhealthy relationship. Maybe she doesn't believe she deserves any better or maybe she's just fearful of being alone.

In short, she's the girl who just doesn't get it—the type most men are *not* looking for.

Could you be that girl?

If you are worried that you may be that girl or have exhibited some of these behaviors in the past, don't despair. You are far from alone. Millions upon millions of women have been that girl and lived to change and even laugh about it. Remember, admitting that you may have a problem is the first step to finding a solution. So have faith and keep reading.

I'm going to talk about *that* girl—or rather *those* girls—throughout this book. And when I get on a roll, don't worry, it's just the guy in me venting. The same guy who so often wants to scream, "Why are you acting like this?!" These parts of the book will shed light on those maladaptive aspects of your personality that can potentially sabotage your ability to have a meaningful, fulfilling relationship.

Then there's the doctor side of me. The doctor who believes that...

If It's Broke, Let's Fix It

When I find that something is wrong, the doctor in me wants to fix it. Sometimes, I walk by a mother with her child and I'll hear the way her son is coughing. All I want to do at that point is go up to the mother and say, "Give him a dose of Decadron and soon he'll start feeling much better." I feel exactly the same way when I see a woman:

- canceling her plans for the evening because the guy who hadn't called all week suddenly decided he wanted to see her;
- going on and on about some guy with whom she's only had one date;
- making excuses and rationalizations so she doesn't

have to stop seeing a guy who is treating her poorly;
- talking about marriage within the first three months of a relationship;
- getting breast implants to get her ex-boyfriend back;
- feeling embarrassed and blaming herself when relationships aren't working out.

So while standards and practices prevent me from approaching the mother about her child, there is nothing to stop me from giving you my honest diagnosis about what you're doing wrong and how you can stop being *that* girl once and for all.

I've been fortunate in my life, whether it be as a friend, as a doctor, or as a boyfriend, to meet many different types of women. I've had countless discussions with female friends, girlfriends, colleagues, and patients about relationships and the male-female dynamic. We've analyzed our current romances over coffee. We've rehashed previous nights' dates over lunch. And we've had plenty of alcohol-fueled conversations about our latest breakups over dinner. In the process, I've come to understand a lot about how women think and why some of you are struggling so much in the relationship department.

And, of course, there was my stint as *The Bachelor*. Talk about an education. I don't think anything can prepare you for the experience of going on a date with twenty-five different women all at once. It definitely forced me to develop a knack for distinguishing sincerity from insincerity and what's endearing from what's not.

One thing I know for certain: If you are able to develop self-confidence and become independently happy, no man can ever take that away from you. In fact, no man worth having in your life will ever *want* to take that away from you. Confidence is sexy.

If you want to hear some practical advice on how to develop that self-confidence, you'll find plenty to help you in the following pages. Pointing out what's wrong is only half the battle. This book will also provide a prescription to benefit you in your pursuit of happiness in life.

Notice how I didn't say "in your pursuit of a man." After all, this book is all about you. So, while the following pages will tell you *why* he may not be that into you, much more important, they will also explain why it's essential to become the kind of woman who isn't particularly concerned about whether he's into you or not. Because if you're into you, that's enough. That's more than enough.

Understanding that men (at least the good ones) are attracted to women who believe in themselves will hopefully energize you to develop habits that lead to more meaningful and fulfilling relationships. And if you believe in yourself, trust me, he'll know.

What Guys Can Tell Just By Looking at You . . .

Believe it or not, at this point in my life, I can look at a woman and tell if she's taken three hours too many to get ready for our date. I can tell if she's listening to what I'm saying or thinking about what she's going to say next. I know if she's trying to impress me by putting on an act or actually being herself. I can see if she's sizing me up for a groom's tux or reserving judgment until she gets to know me better. And that's just the beginning.

I'm not alone. Whether consciously or not, most guys can get a read on a woman as quickly as many of you can look at a guy and figure out whether he's single, gay, or in a relationship, just by the way he looks (or doesn't look) at you. Now, for some of you this information may not be any cause for alarm, but please believe me when I tell you that many of you should be concerned. Very concerned.

Why? Because when a guy looks at you, he sees exactly what you're trying to hide. I can tell if you're in a panic because you feel like your clock is ticking or because your best friend just tied the knot. I sense if you're unsure of yourself and need my approval before you can have a favorable opinion of yourself. I see if you're bored to death with your life and looking to me to provide you with some much-needed excitement. In short, as men, we can tell whether or not you are comfortable and happy with yourself. If we observe something isn't quite right, we sit back and try to figure out whether or not we can live with it or if it may be best just to move on.

Sometimes we can live with it. For instance, I don't care if you're not the best of drivers or not a particularly impressive chess player. I couldn't care less if you don't make a habit of reading the *New York Times* from front to back. And it certainly wouldn't bother me if you gained a few pounds. After all, we are all human and nobody is perfect.

But—and this is a biggie—if you're finding your relationships to be less than satisfying or they don't often go too far past the first few dates or first few months, then this book is for you. If you're constantly complaining that all men are jerks, that no one wants to commit, that all the good ones are taken, and that dating is a nightmare, you are doing something wrong. I guarantee it.

Those GIRLS

As I've already alluded, I've met a wide variety of women in my life. The ones who are happy and fulfilled do not fall into any of the following categories:

1. Agenda Girl: This type of woman is obsessed with getting married. She has a five-year plan that sounds something like this: Meet the right guy within a year. Get married within three. Have a baby in five. Game over. I win. And we live happily ever after.

2. Yes Girl: The Yes Girl cannot agree enough with everything her date or boyfriend says. In fact, she's the girl who is always going along with things in order to get along. While these girls are fun at first, the lack of conflict gets old real quick.

3. Drama Queen Girl: This woman has taken the motto "follow your heart" a little too literally, getting overly emotional about every possible aspect of a relationship, past and present— from the cute guy who just sent her a message on MySpace to the ex-boyfriend who broke up with her three years ago. Give me a break!

4. Bitter Girl: This type of woman is holding on to a grudge. Unfortunately, it's against the entire male population. She's been hurt before and she's going to make sure that it never happens again. Taking the idea that the best defense is a good offense way too far, Bitter Girl alienates men with her behavior wherever she goes.

5. Insecure Girl: This type of woman is painfully self-conscious. She may be unsure about her looks, her intelligence, or her sense of humor, but usually neither her looks nor her personality are as unattractive as her lack of self-confidence. She's often the girl who needs a few drinks as her social crutch.

6. Desperate Girl: This is the girl who will phone-stalk a guy until she gets his attention. She absolutely will not be ignored. Sound familiar? Like something out of *Fatal Attraction*, maybe? While the real life Desperate Girl is probably nowhere near as bad as Glenn Close, she's definitely the inspiration for the character.

7. Working Girl: Most of us need to work, but this type of woman really makes a federal case out of it. She hides behind her career, using it as an excuse to get out of the intimidating world of dating and relationships and is often heard saying that she doesn't need a relationship because she's too busy with her job.

8. Lost Girl: This is the woman who finds herself "lost" in an unhealthy relationship but doesn't have the strength or capacity to walk away. She may have all of her ducks in a row outside of the relationship, but when it comes to her boyfriend, she's a real mess. She'll rationalize why he cheated or why he treats her poorly and she'll pull out the "if you only knew him the way I know him" crap. At least she's not alone . . . or is she?

Like the title says, DON'T BE THAT GIRL! If you fit into any of these categories, you may get into a relationship and you may get married, but, to put it bluntly, you probably won't be doing it with a very smart, stable, or solid guy. Take it from me, all the sensible men I know steer clear of these types of women when it comes to long-term, serious commitments. And if a healthy relationship is what you really want, your first step is to admit that you're having a problem getting it.

The following chapters will help you zero in on your problem areas and figure out how they are getting in the way of what you want. We will discuss the qualities of the eight types of women you absolutely, positively do not want to be and provide both long-term and short-term solutions to help you stop acting crazy right here and now. At the same time, I will show you how to structure your life so that you are not a walking, talking man-repellant. But we're getting ahead of ourselves. . . . Let's begin by figuring out whether you could be that girl and not even know it!

COULD YOU BE That GIRL?

You may have read over the list and thought: *Phew! That doesn't sound anything like me. I'm just fine. Like I said, it's the guys who are crazy.* If that sounds about right, then please trust me when I tell you that you could very well be *that* girl. Some of the women who could benefit the most from this book are unfortunately the least likely to think they need it. That's why, before we begin, take a moment to consider the following:

1. Are you alone but longing for a boyfriend?
2. Are you in an unsatisfying or unhealthy relationship?
3. Are you still not really sure why your last boyfriend broke up with you?
4. Would your friends say you act differently when you're in a relationship?
5. Have you found that guys don't seem to want to commit to you?
6. Have you pursued many men who have not reciprocated your interest?
7. Are you generally unhappy with the state of your life right now?

If your answers to *any* of the above questions are yes, then keep reading. You may have more in common with these types of women than you think.

Agenda Girl

You probably know at least one Agenda Girl. I certainly have met enough to consider myself something of an expert on the kind of woman who asks me how many children I'd like and if I could ever see myself settling down (and when) during our second date—or sooner. I once had a woman ask me during the first thirty minutes of our first date if I was ready for marriage and children because she felt like her clock was ticking and she didn't want to waste her time with men who weren't "serious" about dating. Take it from a guy, that is *not* how you want to start off your first date.

The Agenda Girl is the one who's been planning her wedding since she was old enough to count to ten bridesmaids. Her hobbies include reading *Modern Bride* and designing her dream engagement ring on adiamondisforever.com. (Don't ask me how I know this!) She secretly seethes with envy every time another friend gets engaged, but is first in line for the bouquet toss at the wedding. She's known exactly how many children she wants as well as at what age she wants to have them since she was fifteen—unfortunately, she hasn't revised those ideas since. She has a list of requirements for her potential husband that is at least a mile long, although, in case of emergency (e.g. she's twenty-nine and still not married), she will gladly settle for someone who allows her to check her top five boxes:

☑ - decent looks
☑ - advanced degree in a prestigious profession
☑ - steady job in a lucrative field (what's the use of a law degree if you're just going to waste it at a nonprofit?)
☑ - good family
☑ - ready to settle down

There you have it, everything an Agenda Girl needs for a real, honest-to-goodness fairy-tale romance. And guess what? I can tell all this about her within an hour of our first date. How? Because that is usually how long it takes her to decide whether or not she wants to start grooming me for the role of Mr. Agenda Girl.

Of course, not every Agenda Girl is quite that obvious. Plenty of women enter into relationships with open minds only to find themselves getting hung up on the idea of marriage before the time is ripe—meaning, before their boyfriend is ready. In these cases, the relationship often self-destructs when the agenda comes to light in the form of premature demands and a relationship-ending ultimatum.

Could You Be an Agenda Girl?

Even if you're nowhere near as extreme as the girl I just described, Agenda Girls come in all shapes and sizes. Answer these true/false questions to find out if the bridal shoe fits . . . and be honest!

1. **T / F**   I am almost always the one who introduces the subject of marriage and children.

2. **T / F**   I often find myself thinking about what we'll do on future dates during our first few outings.

3. **T / F**   I have actually practiced signing my name using my boyfriend's last name.

4. **T / F**   I feel sorry for the losers, er, I mean women, who are over thirty and still not married.

5. **T / F**   My biological clock sounds more like a ticking time bomb. If I don't have children within the next few years, I'll explode.

6. **T / F**   My first dates are usually a lot like job interviews.

7. **T / F**   If I don't get married by a certain age, I'll feel like an old maid.

8. **T / F**   It is important for me to figure out fairly quickly whether or not I would marry a guy.

9. **T / F**   If my boyfriend didn't propose to me within eighteen months, I would leave and find someone who would.

10. **T / F**   *The Rules* is my dating bible.

Scoring:

0-2 True: While you want to get married eventually, you are not turning guys off with an obvious marriage agenda.

3-5 True: So maybe you don't have your imaginary babies' names all picked out, but what you do have is a minor case of Agenda Girlitis. Take my word, even a minor case can be a major relationship killer, so read on.

6+ True: You are a full-blown Agenda Girl. Please keep reading to learn how you can stop driving men away.

Two Reasons Why Guys Don't Like Agenda Girls

A premature wedding agenda is such a turnoff that even the worst offenders know better than to reveal their true intentions. Unfortunately, trying to hide the truth from a date is nearly impossible if you don't believe your own story. So next time you're sitting there, spinning some yarn about how you're in no rush to get married—all the while mentally calculating how long it will take to get this guy to fall for you so you can spring the truth on him—understand this: Any guy with eyes can see right through your hidden agenda.

I know what you're thinking. *And? So what? What is so wrong with wanting to get married?*

Absolutely nothing. Again, the problem with Agenda Girl isn't that she wants to get married, it's that she wants to get married to anyone who fits her requirements and will pop the question by the date circled in her meticulously organized day planner. Which leads me to the first reason men don't like the Agenda Girl:

Reason #1: We want to feel special too.

Believe it or not, men have feelings. We want to feel special and appreciated for our unique qualities. We want to feel like we have forged an uncommon connection with the person we're dating. Like we've found something precious and rare—someone who gets us and loves us for who we are. Unfortunately, it's painfully clear that Agenda Girl doesn't much care how we feel, what we want, or who we are. All she cares about is how we'll fit in with *her* plan, *her* dreams, and *her* life.

Here's how the typical guy will respond to an obvious Agenda Girl. First, he'll feel flattered that you're so obviously into him that you want to marry him. *Wow,* he'll think, *I must be a real catch.*

One minute later, that feeling will pass and he'll start thinking: *What's wrong with this woman? Why is she so in love with me when she doesn't even know me? What does she want from me? Ah! She's not in love with me at all. It has nothing to do with me. She just wants to get married. Oh boy . . . not again!*

"Check please!"

Despite what some Agenda Girls may think, this typical reaction does not mean that the guy is immature or unable to commit. He just doesn't want to commit to you.

Put yourself into our shoes for a minute. After all, women don't have a monopoly on agendas. Guys can be just as guilty. Except in the guy's case, the agenda may be sex, not marriage.

Take a moment to think back to a time when a date's behavior made it quite obvious that all he really cared about was getting some action. Any number of things may have tipped you off. It could have been the way his eyes glazed over when he stared deep into your cleavage. Maybe it was his won't-take-no-for-an-answer insistence that you order that third frozen margarita. Or perhaps you had reason to pause after the fifth time he told you how you're the smartest, sexiest, most charming and beautiful woman he'd ever met. We all love compliments, but if you were able to see this behavior for what it really was—a full-court press to get you into bed—chances are the resulting ego boost didn't last very long.

When a guy makes his intentions so obvious, it's only natural that you stop to think, *Hmm, I wonder if he says this to all the girls?*

Guess what? Guys feel the same way when a woman is working an agenda of her own. No matter what the agenda, the man who is just trying to enjoy your company, go with the flow, and get to know you better is going to catch on. And when that happens, don't be surprised if your text messages start going unanswered.

Reason #2: We want surprises.

Surprise and mystery are at the core of romance. Guys want and need to spend some time wondering, *Does she like me too?* No, women aren't the only ones who sometimes turn to the Magic 8 Ball. We want to feel emotionally invested, and since every investment involves some risk of losing, we cannot feel invested when you are a sure thing and we are 100 percent certain of your intentions. It just doesn't work that way.

The problem with the Agenda Girl is that she cannot tolerate the level of uncertainty that's necessary for a real relationship to blossom. Afraid of the risks that come with true romance, she prefers to look at a relationship like a job. Except in this case, she's reaching for the diamond ring, not the brass one.

To attain her goal, Agenda Girl sets up signposts to guide her along the road to the altar. Any guy who is dating one of these girls suddenly feels like he's been hired for a new job. And he knows exactly what is expected of him:

1. Friday or Saturday night dates for the first few months.
2. Pressure to stop seeing other people.
3. Drawer space.
4. Those "three little words" before the fourth month. Often followed by the horrifying . . . "Don't you feel the same way?" response to our silence.
5. Meeting each other's parents as soon as possible.
6. A ring within eighteen months or less. Or an ultimatum.
7. Either marry her and be miserable, or break if off and make her miserable.

Not only does the typical Agenda Girl relationship usually lead to either a breakup or an unhappily ever after, but, as you can see, the journey to the altar isn't much fun for the guy involved. Like I said, zero surprises. We know exactly what Agenda Girl will do every step of the way. If she gets what she wants, she'll be flush with success and giddily lavish us with affection. If she doesn't, we'll never hear the end of it. She'll nag, she'll turn on the waterworks, she'll threaten to leave. . . . She'll make our lives a living hell. Call me crazy, call me immature, call me commitment phobic, just don't call me Ms. Agenda's boyfriend. No thanks!

The Dead Giveaways

Maybe I shouldn't be telling you this, but there are two ways in which Agenda Girls tip us off every time. I am not revealing this information so you can better hide your agenda. Hopefully, by the time you're through with this chapter, and the book, you'll see why you're much better off approaching every relationship with an open mind (e.g. Who knows what will happen? We could end up as a couple, as friends, or even as in-laws!) instead of with a specific goal in mind (e.g. I will make him fall in love with me and marry me). In the meantime, keep in mind that if you are unilaterally hatching a marriage plot, you will almost certainly be compelled to act in one of the following off-putting ways.

Dead Giveaway #1: The Third Degree

"We were set up by mutual friends. I already knew he was great on paper based on what they'd told me—twenty-nine years old. Went to Exeter for high school. Princeton undergrad. MBA from Wharton. Investment banker. I was so excited, I spent all day getting ready. Hair. Nails. Mystic tan. A new dress. I have to say, I was looking hot! At dinner, the more questions I asked, the better he looked: Apartment in the city. House in the country. Audi TT Roadster (a personal favorite!). On good terms with

his mother and father (who, by the way, are both very prominent Boston lawyers). Two past long-term relationships. Tired of the bar scene. All that *and* a face that wouldn't ruin the family photos. I was ready to marry him right then and there! He walked me home and we hugged and did that whole peck on the cheek thing. Then I never heard from him again. *We would have made the perfect couple! What is wrong with guys today?!"*
—Karen, 26, New York, NY

"What's wrong with guys?" Good question. The only thing is I have a hunch that if Karen really wanted to know the answer, she would have spent at least some part of her date getting to know her future husband instead of ratcheting up his list of accomplishments and imagining what their kids would look like while watching his lips move. Something tells me that even with all her questions, by the end of her date, Karen still had absolutely no insight into this so-called perfect man's personality. All she really cared about was that he looked good "on paper" (an expression that, by the way, is universally despised by the guys I know).

Take it from me, I've been in this position more than enough times to know what Karen's date was thinking: *Why does this girl remind me so much of those nosey people on my co-op board? Wait a second, I know what she's getting at. She's checking to see if I'm marriage material. She's got her sights on me and I don't even know her yet. Chances are she'll just wind up falling for me and I'm going to end up hurting her. Let's stop this ride right here.*

And that's just what the decent guy would do. We'll get into what another type of guy would do later in the chapter.

All I'm saying is, whoa . . . slow down. Just because a guy has the right car, hairstyle, or college degree—or even the trifecta—

doesn't mean he is meant for you. He's no dummy; he can tell by your line of questioning and that lovestruck look in your eyes that you're looking to take the relationship to the next level. And if you're an Agenda Girl, you're probably getting excited and trying to move things along way too soon. Then the pressure is on, adrenaline kicks in, and a guy is left with only two choices: fight or flight. Now, if you've heard it once, you must have heard it a million times: Men hate confrontation. So we flee.

Dead Giveaway #2: Laying Down the Law

"I am serious about getting married. And I want my dates to know that right off the bat. So I tell them up front, 'I am not into sport dating. I am looking for a serious relationship.' I am also very honest about what I will and will not tolerate. For instance, I tell them that if they say they'll call the next day, that means the next day. Not the next evening. Not the next night. And certainly not the day after the next. I can't stand flakes!"
—Mary, 29, Seattle, WA

You could be the most beautiful woman in the entire city, but if you approach the men you meet with Mary's brutally honest, no-nonsense, take-no-prisoners attitude you will only succeed in scaring off the good ones. I know it's only too tempting to rationalize that sort of behavior by telling yourself you're sick of playing games and you want to be straightforward. But please, just for one moment, imagine how you would feel if a guy you'd only known for a week or so told you that he was a one-woman man and he expected a one-man woman, so if you're dating around, well, this just isn't going to work for him. If you're not a little afraid, then I am afraid for you. No grown adult should be told how to act or what to do—much less by a near-perfect stranger. I don't care how sexy that stranger may be. If a woman doesn't understand that a relationship needs to progress to the next level naturally, she will scare away almost any worthwhile guy she meets. We do want commitment and we do want loyalty, but we're not ready for that discussion after only one week.

During the course of any relationship, be it a romance, a friendship, or a professional partnership, we have to earn the privilege of being able to make demands. But Agenda Girl doesn't want to waste a whole lot of time paying all the pesky dues that go hand in hand with an entry-level romance. Blinded by the glare of her future engagement ring, Agenda Girl cannot see past what she wants, and she will say whatever is on her mind. If the guy doesn't like it, she'll go look for someone else who will.

Most guys I know are only too happy to let her go ahead and do that.

A DATE IS NOT AN INTERVIEW

I don't think you can have a more painful experience than a date that feels like a job interview. Or a marriage interview. Or any type of interview, for that matter. The problem is that when you have an agenda, a date often does resemble an interview. How do I know this? Let's just say I've been guilty of my own agendas.

In college, I went on a date with a girl many considered to be the most beautiful on campus. I went out with her with one goal to accomplish: get the girl. Unfortunately, since I was so focused on an agenda rather than trying to get to know her as an individual, the date was doomed. At dinner, I was extremely nervous and all I could think was: *This is going horribly.* The conversation was perfunctory and I brought absolutely no charm to the table. Zilch. I was boring, nervous, and I don't think I gave a hearty laugh or offered a genuine smile during our entire dinner conversation. Instead I kept falling back on questions that led to one-word answers and my true personality disappeared. Guess how that date ended? A "thanks for dinner," a polite peck on the cheek, and the occasional awkward "hello" on campus until I finally graduated.

After that date, I vowed never to allow an agenda or the interview mentality to encroach upon my dating life ever again. I now approach each and every date I go on with a completely different attitude. This is about pleasure, not business. I'm excited to have fun, to laugh, and to get to know my date, not interview her or be interviewed.

We've all been on the brutal interview date. It usually goes something like:

> Guy: So what do you do?
> Girl: I'm an accountant.
> Guy: Cool.
> Girl: What do you do?
> Guy: I'm a photographer.
> Girl: Cool.
> Guy: Where do you live?
> Girl and Guy: Zzz . . . zzz . . . zzz

Whether you're the interviewer or the interviewee, you can turn things around if you realize this is how your date is going. Rescue yourself (or your date) by taking the following measures:

1. Ask open-ended questions: Asking these types of questions leads to interesting conversation instead of one word answers. For example:

What was your college experience like?

instead of

Where did you go to college?

What do you enjoy most about your job?

instead of

What is your job?

2. Ask follow-up questions: Follow up any objective question with one that will allow you to legitimately get to know your date. For instance, after you ask him if he has any siblings and he says, "Yes, a sister," instead of simply nodding your head and saying "Ah, that's nice," try coming back with a probing question or two, such as: What is your sister like? Do you get along well? Or better yet, explore his aspirations by asking him, if he could do anything, what would it be?

If, despite a sweet resume, he has no legitimate aspirations or his answers reveal he's a psycho, maybe *you* should be the one asking for the check. (At least later when your friends ask how your date went you'll have a more interesting answer than "eh, fine.") Regardless, always listen to what he says rather than staring longingly into your future husband's eyes. Don't get ahead of yourself—you're just getting to know him. And don't forget to have fun!

BEHIND THE AGENDA

Anyone who is dead set on getting married before she's even met the right guy probably has a reason for it. Too bad most of the time that reason sounds something like this:

1. Because I'm thirty-three and it's high time. Everyone has their own path to follow. Just because you're a certain age doesn't mean you should be married.

2. To prove I'm not a reject. Many women view having a

boyfriend as proof of their desirability. After all, if one guy wants you, you can't be all bad, right? Wrong.

3. Marriage will solve all my problems. Blaming your issues on being single and thinking that marriage is some kind of a cure-all will only ensure that you find a whole new set of complaints after the honeymoon.

4. I don't want to die alone. If you're afraid of winding up alone, it may be wiser to start out by forging some solid friendships before forcing a relationship. A marriage certificate is not insurance against winding up alone.

5. All my friends are married. Being the last single on the block may not always be the most fun position to occupy, but if you think keeping up with your friends' marital status is reason enough to get married, think again.

6. He's a great catch! Just because a guy is all-around wonderful doesn't mean that he's the perfect guy for you. Even if everyone else thinks you've caught the big one, you won't be happy if the compatibility isn't there.

7. I want kids while I'm young. That's great. So did Britney Spears, and look how that turned out. Make sure you understand what you're getting into before you try turning your life into a Norman Rockwell painting.

8. To wear that dress! Go to the store, try it on, take pictures, and then forget it. If this is really a major reason you want to get married, we have our work cut out for us.

The Dangers of an Agenda

Ever hear the warning, "Be careful what you wish for . . . you just might get it"? Well, working in the ER, I have seen firsthand the damage that an agenda can wreak upon women's lives. The idea that a wedding is an end in and of itself can lead to a great deal of heartbreak when the reality fails to live up to the fairy-tale notion of happily ever after. I have seen women who were so disappointed and depressed once they got the lives they always thought they wanted that they turned to alcohol, drugs, and even suicide as a means to cope, rebel, or escape.

Now I'm not saying that all marriages are bad. Far from it. If both people understand the nature of this serious commitment and what it entails, marriage can be a wonderful thing. But marriage can also feel like a death sentence when it hasn't been well thought out or when two people aren't compatible. I can't tell you how many women have been driven to the brink of despair because they've got the house, the kids, the cars, and the security, but they're still unhappy—and they don't know why. The fact is, sometimes women who are stuck on getting married may think they know what they want, when in fact they are building their entire lives around a fantasy of wedded bliss. Unfortunately, they forget that a wedding equals bliss only if they are blessed with the right partner.

Don't Date That Guy

The biggest problem with being an Agenda Girl is not that you send most guys packing. If you can believe it, being alone is nothing compared to being with the type of guy who is actually attracted to an Agenda Girl. It never fails—any Agenda Girl who stumbles her way into a relationship is bound to wind up with one of these guys:

- **Mr. Yes Dear:** The weak, spineless guy who cannot stand to be alone is a prime target for Agenda Girl. He's boring, and has few ideas of his own to conflict with your agenda. Sure, he's only too happy to jump through any hoops you set up for him, but not necessarily because he loves you. It's because he'd rather go along with whatever you want than assert himself. Can you respect that?

- **Mr. I'll Put Up with Anything for Steady Sex:** This type of guy lacks all sexual confidence and will stay with you because he doesn't think he can get anyone else to go to bed with him. That, and he's lazy. Sure, he'll be faithful, but if that sounds like the foundation of a beautiful friendship to you, you're selling yourself short.

- **Mr. Agenda Guy:** He's got the job. He's got the house. Now all he needs is the little woman to produce some offspring and his life will be perfect. Except, it doesn't much matter to him whether or not you two connect on any level other than your mutual desire for a family and a country club membership, so you're almost certainly guaranteed plenty of boring nights, eating dinner in silence in front of the plasma TV.

- **Mr. Master Manipulator:** These guys are smooth talkers. They're smart and they know *exactly* what an Agenda Girl is thinking. But instead of being annoyed or turned off by your secret schemes and plans, the Master Manipulator has figured out how to make your agenda work for him. He'll look deep into your eyes and tell you exactly what you need to hear to get you into bed. It may last a few months, a few weeks, or a few hours. But as soon as he's had enough sex, he's gone. Hey, all's fair in love and war, right?

ARE YOU IN THE WAITING LINE?

So many of the women I meet seem to spend their single years in a perpetual state of limbo, constantly waiting for something to happen. For Mr. Right to come knocking. For those three little words. For the proposal. For the wedding. For the children. Always waiting for real life to begin. If this is your attitude, it's no wonder you're not living your life to the fullest.

Take it from a guy. . . . We have a completely different attitude toward our single years. We see this as our time to have fun, to do outrageous things, to live out the adventures that people who are married with children can only read about. We're trying to get all the fun out of our system before we get married so that when we do settle down, we're not sitting around thinking, *It's too bad I never got the chance to travel and be more spontaneous before I had kids.*

If being single is your favorite excuse for putting off living your life and doing what you want to do, some of the following may sound familiar:

1. "I'd love to go to Brazil, but I want my next vacation to be with my boyfriend!"
2. "Sure it would be nice to invest in home décor, but what if I go to all the trouble of decorating and then have to move out because I've met someone?"
3. "I'm really into cooking/dance/tennis and would love to take a class, but I'm not doing it without a boyfriend."
4. "Sure, it would make sense to buy a condo, but what if I get married and have to sell?"
5. "I could see myself going back to school, but I think I should really be concentrating on meeting a husband."

Now if any of that sounds even remotely like you, then what will you bring to your relationship when you finally do meet a guy you like? After all, before you can start jet-setting around the world and shopping for home furnishings together, you'll have to impress him with your personality, your character, and your life experiences. And that's going to seem like one tall order if you're living your life in limbo. So think about what you're interested in or passionate about and pursue it. If you've ever heard someone talking about a hobby or activity that sounded fun, give it a shot. You'll feel more independent and confident—and it will show.

Before You Jump Off a Bridge . . .

I'll admit I haven't exactly gone easy in this chapter. But if you could see the Agenda Girl the way most guys do, you would understand that if anything, I haven't been harsh enough. Please understand that my only goal is to get you to stop putting the cart before the horse when you're out there dating. While having an agenda is great in school and in business, Agenda Girls are their own worst enemies in all matters related to love and relationships. Of course, none of this is to say that being an Agenda Girl is all bad. So before you start hitting yourself over the head with that wedding scrapbook you started keeping in junior high, consider all the positive qualities that you have to offer the world:

- **Goal-oriented:** The world is driven by focused, disciplined people who believe in reaching for their dreams. And you are just such a person.
- **Strong:** You have the courage of your convictions. You know what you want, and you go for it.

- **Determined:** Undeterred by obstacles, you keep trying to accomplish the tasks you set for yourself. A sure recipe for success in life, if not always in relationships.
- **Family-minded:** You're maternal and place a high value on family. Nothing wrong with that!

In short, there's nothing wrong with you for wanting to get married, have kids, and raise a warm, loving family. That only makes you human. We all want happy families of our own. My only concern is for those of you who allow this desire to become such an all-consuming need that it overrides every other aspect of your personality—not to mention your life—and turns you into the dreaded Agenda Girl.

Your Rx: Find a New Agenda

Since you are so goal-oriented and driven, your best bet to overcoming your marriage agenda would be to replace it with an entirely new, more productive agenda. If you become happy with your life, you won't have to be on the constant lookout for the marriage escape hatch. Ultimately, *that* is what is going to lead you to a good relationship, not the relentless pursuit of a husband.

Finding fulfillment in your work, your friendships, and/or your hobbies will contribute to a happier and more desirable you. Think about it, who's got time to become neurotic and obsessive when so much of her energy is going toward something that has absolutely nothing to do with dating and relationships?

Here are three new potential agendas that will help you forget all about how desperately you want to get married:

1. Employee of the Year: Now, shocking as this may sound, I've met Agenda Girls who have put all their energies into achieving wedded bliss just to get out of careers they hate. I've also met some who assumed that they shouldn't get invested in their jobs because marriage and children would eventually take them away from all that. To quit being an Agenda Girl, you'll have to stop thinking along these lines. Marriage is neither a sure thing nor a Get Out of Work Free card. It's not going to solve all your career and money problems. On the other hand, shaping up your professional life will. You can start immediately by putting in more effort at work for the next year so you can get a promotion. You can also spend your free hours looking for a new job in a field you're interested in or taking classes that will help you land your dream job.

2. Better health: If you make physical fitness a priority, you'll find that you're way too busy taking good care of yourself to spend much time thinking about how you can manipulate Mr. Right into popping the question. So cross off "Get Married" on your mental to-do list, and replace it with "Get in Shape." Improving your health can mean anything from increasing your physical activity to changing your eating habits to quitting smoking. But once you start on the path to feeling good, you're likely to find that it's hard to stop midway. After you've quit your bad habits, don't be surprised if the time you used to spend worrying about being single is now taken up with working out, preparing quality meals, and just feeling all around great about your energy levels and state of mind.

3. Friendship First: Our friendships are practice for the more involved, romantic relationships we forge with our partners. If you're finding that loneliness is forcing you deep into a state of Agenda Girl territory, take it as a sign to reconnect with your friends or make some new ones. Go ahead and put "Become More Social" at the top of your Agenda. Then, start expanding your circle by calling up people you may not have seen in a while and asking them to grab a cup of coffee or go out to lunch together. Remember, the qualities that make you a good friend are the same as the ones that will make you a great significant other.

You don't have to look high and low to find the missing link that will make your life great. You already have everything you need to be happy, be that your work, your hobbies, or your friends and/or family. Once you start working on making the most of what you have, you'll find that you have less time to chase the things you don't. In the end, a man or marriage is not something you should ever chase. In fact, you are most likely to find what you're looking for when you stop chasing it.

Fake It Till You Make It

In this chapter hopefully I've provided you with some reasons to combat your agenda issues for a long time to come. But I wouldn't be much of a friend if I didn't also give some quick tips to help you out right here and now. So even if you're not ready to say good-bye to your career as an amateur wedding planner just yet, here are some immediate, Band-Aid solutions to help you stop laying all your cards on the table and losing out in the dating game:

- **Steer clear of these taboo subjects while on a date with a new guy:** Your next date, commitment, marriage, and children. Whatever you do, don't be the one who brings up any of these topics. I'm not going to go into any more details as to why. I think I covered all that in the course of this chapter. All that's left for you to do is to take my advice and cut a wide swath around these subjects.

- **Tear up your list of must-have qualities in a husband (or at least hide it away where no one will find it!),** and write a new list of things you want to do before having kids. Start chipping away at it right now.
- **Stop planning ahead.** If you catch yourself making long-term plans for you and the guy you just met three weeks ago, stop immediately to consider that you two may very well not make it to next week, much less next year.
- **Focus on friendship:** Instead of going on dates with the intention of bagging a husband, think about each date as an opportunity to meet someone who may become a good friend or teach you something new. This should help you keep an open, clear-headed perspective.
- **Take a three-month vacation from your husband hunting.** See what happens when you banish all thoughts of your future wedding, husband, and children from your mind.

Last but not least, do not—and I mean this—ever, under any circumstances, tell a guy that your eggs are rotting or that the only reason to get married is to have kids. Got it?

Yes Girl

As I said from the beginning, this book is not a manual on boyfriend hunting and this particular chapter will prove my point. The truth about Yes Girls is that they frequently get the guy. In fact, lots of men love the Yes Girl. And why not? Think about it, if you were out with someone who laughed at all your jokes, enthusiastically agreed with all your opinions, and wanted to do all the same activities you did, wouldn't you feel like maybe you'd struck pay dirt?

Sure you would—at least for a little while. The satisfaction of having found someone who seems to share all your values and appreciates exactly how wonderful you are could last anywhere from one hour to one year, but eventually, the reality will sink in and disappointment won't be long in coming. As it turns out, you haven't found your soul mate—you've just wound up with someone who is way too eager to please.

Although she is the polar opposite of the Agenda Girl, the Yes Girl is no less dysfunctional. While the Agenda Girl ignores the needs of her dates and boyfriends in order to fit them into her life and her plans, the Yes Girl neglects her own needs and wishes to fit into the life of whomever she is dating.

To say that I've met a couple of Yes Girls in my time would be a vast understatement. Not only have I dated a few, but I've also seen many good friends jump on the Yes Girl bandwagon as well. Take my friend Andrea for example. When I met Andrea, we were both undergrads at Duke University. At the time, she was a conscientious, straight-*A* student and had a clean-cut, preppy style. One night, a group of us went out in Durham to hear a local band play. Andrea and the drummer hit it off after the concert. Within a month, she had acquired a new tattoo, a nose piercing, and more than a couple of failing grades on papers and exams. Her explanation? She was "in love." I don't know how she managed to scrape by that semester, but the following year, she was no longer involved with the drummer and back to acting like her old self—albeit with a tattoo that didn't quite fit her personality.

Then there's my friend Samantha. The first time she tried online dating, she showed me the profile she'd written and I could barely contain my laughter. None of it sounded anything like her. For instance, she was not the Colorado Rockies-loving baseball fan she made herself out to be. Nor was she a particularly skilled snowboarder, despite what the picture of her holding a snowboard might have led one to believe. When I asked her what in the world she'd been thinking, she basically told me that that's what she thought guys were looking for.

And that's the Yes Girl for you. She is the woman who becomes exactly who she thinks her boyfriend wants her to be. If he wants a partner in crime, someone who will club hop with him until the sun comes up, she's only too happy to be that person—even if she doesn't particularly like spending all her free time in nightclubs. If her next boyfriend is the traditional type, she will quickly stock her normally empty refrigerator, scour the cookbook section of the nearest bookstore, and obsess over the genius of Martha Stewart. Should her next boyfriend be an avid camper, she'll invest in hypnotherapy to overcome her fear of bugs and join him in the great outdoors every weekend.

But who is the Yes Girl at heart? What does she really like to do? How does she actually feel? No one knows, either because the Yes Girl herself is unsure, or because she's too afraid of revealing her opinions to show her true self. She is a chameleon who changes personas and lifestyles faster than you can say rebound relationship. And I'm not talking about the woman who picks up golf or surfing because she's always been curious and now that she's dating a guy who can teach her, she's all over it. No, I am talking about the girl whose actual style, habits, and preferences all change in response to the man in her life.

Sound familiar? Do yourself a favor and find out if you're this girl because the whole Stepford girlfriend act is nowhere near as attractive—or, more important, gratifying—as being a woman who knows who she is, what she wants, and how to express herself in a confident, positive way.

Could You Be a Yes Girl?

Everyone knows that the first step to overcoming any problem is to admit you have one. Since you can't very well fess up to an issue you may not even know you have, take this quiz and find out if you're a Yes Girl:

1. If your long-term boyfriend decided to move cross-country for a job and asked you to come with him, you would:
   a. Tell him to have a great life, but you can't imagine leaving

your job and all of your wonderful friends.

b. Start looking for apartments and making all the arrangements for your life in the new city.

c. Have some serious thinking to do.

2. On your second date with a guy you really like, he says that he never wants to get married. If you are looking to settle down, what is your reaction?

a. Wish him well in life.

b. Say nothing. Who knows? Maybe he's right. Maybe marriage is overrated, even though you've always thought you would like to get married.

c. Talk about it casually, but then re-evaluate whether or not you want to continue seeing him.

3. Your manager leaves work early every other day, comes in late all the time, and then gets annoyed when you dare to ask to leave one hour early. You react by:

a. Leaving one hour early. Who cares if that hypocrite is annoyed?

b. Forgoing your plans and staying until the end of the day.

c. Getting his/her approval by volunteering to skip lunch, then embarking on a job search. You don't know how much longer you'll be able to work for someone like that.

4. Your girlfriend is moving to a new apartment. She calls to ask if you would help her with the move, but you have a networking event scheduled for that day and you are really looking forward to it. You:

a. *Excuse* me? What kind of a question is this? No friend of yours would ever ask you to help them move. They know better.

b. Agree to help. That's what friends are for.

c. Tell her you have a previous engagement and can't make it, but give her the number of some low-cost movers you know.

5. Who usually picks the restaurant, you or your date?

a. That would be you. You are a genius when it comes to finding all the great places to eat in this city.

b. You leave that stuff to your date to figure out. You would hate to suggest a restaurant he doesn't like.

c. Hmm, You can't really say one way or the other. Sometimes it's you, other times it's him. It all depends on the situation.

6. When you're involved in a long-term relationship, your group of friends is:

a. The same as it ever was. Your friends are your friends. Why would a relationship change that?

b. Mostly new. His friends become your friends. Of course, You still keep your old friends, but you just don't see each other much.

c. Usually a bit larger. Your friends, his friends, who cares? The more the merrier.

7. Your current love interest tells you he liked a movie that you thought was boring. You:

a. Tell him that his taste in movies needs some serious work and proceed to mock him mercilessly.

b. Agree that yes, it was a pretty good movie. In fact, maybe it deserves an Oscar.

c. Say nothing. Everyone knows guys have bad taste in movies. Who cares?

8. Your boyfriend loves to bowl. You think it's a waste of time. You:

a. Question his taste in hobbies and refuse to take any part in that so-called sport.

b. Buy yourself a bowling ball, shoes, and a bag to match. You're sure you'll have fun once he shows you how it's done.

c. Go bowling with him once in a while, but mostly just let him have his nights with the guys at the alley.

9. The sentence you agree with most is:

a. Being right makes me happy.

b. I like a man who takes charge so I don't have to.

c. I know how to pick my battles.

10. When you're in a relationship, your sense of style tends to:

a. Improve. If the guy you're with gets the hint and starts dressing nicer, he just may be a keeper.

b. Mirror your boyfriend's. What's the point of dressing like a fashion plate when you're dating a guy who spends all his time in torn Levi's?

c. Stay the same. You love your clothes. You wouldn't change a thing.

Scoring:

Number you answered with *a*: _____ x 1 = _____

Number you answered with *b*: _____ x 3 = _____

Number you answered with *c*: _____ x 2 = _____

Add up your totals in the last column = _____

10-16 points: Certainly no Yes Girl issues here. Other issues possibly, but you are most definitely not at any man's beck and call. You know your mind and you're not afraid to speak it. However, your tendency to act domineering could mean you're a Bitter Girl, an Agenda Girl, or one of the other types of women I discuss in the chapters that follow. Then again, maybe you're just extremely independent and have no desire for the necessary give and take of a relationship right now. Only you can say for sure.

17-23 points: You have a good sense of your own boundaries, but are open enough to let people in. You know how to assert yourself without stepping on other people's toes and have learned that balance is the key to carrying on healthy, mutually-satisfying relationships.

24-30 points: Your people-pleasing ways have gotten completely out of hand. Being agreeable is all well and good, until you start losing sight of what you really want. You regularly put the needs and desires of others ahead of yourself. While you may think this is winning you the love you want, the truth is that you're letting people take you for granted. Remember, if you can't appreciate yourself and put yourself first, no one else will either—and that includes your significant other.

Two Reasons Why Guys Don't Like Yes Girls

Like I said before, many guys are drawn to Yes Girls. We'll talk about these types a bit later in the chapter. In the meantime, I want to address the ways in which being a Yes Girl can actually wreak havoc when you're trying to carry on a serious long-term relationship with a man of substance. For instance:

Reason #1: Zzzz . . . zzzz . . . zzzz . . . does it have to be so **boring***?!*
While nobody wants a relationship that is one long, drawn-out argument after another, the same goes for the opposite extreme. Some disagreement is not only normal and healthy, it's actually exciting. For instance, there is no way in the world that two people will want to do the same thing all the time. Even if it's just a difference in opinion over what movie to see, you're bound to hit a bump in the road at some point. Temperatures will rise, body heat will escalate, and if you don't wind up in a full-scale argument, you'll at least engage in a mature debate. And even if you do have a full-scale argument, makeup sex may follow.

Unless, of course, you're a Yes Girl, in which case you'll just shrug and say, "Fine, whatever you want to do. Makes no differ-ence to me." Conversation over. Opportunity for "mature debate" squandered.

And that right there is the problem with conflict-free relationships—they're usually passion-free as well. There's no heat or friction. Life becomes one boring, uneventful routine. You act as if it doesn't matter whether you see that Jet Li movie he's had his eye on or that drama you've been interested in for the last three weeks. You say you couldn't care less if he takes you out to that hot new restaurant like he'd promised or if you spend another Friday night preparing a home-cooked meal. Everything is A-okay by you. You act as if you have no interest in getting your way. No fighting spirit. Nothing driving you to assert your-self within the relationship. This Mother Teresa song and dance may work for a while, but pretty soon, hanging out with you becomes about as interesting as listening to a clock tick as the relationship goes bust.

As men, we end up spending a lot of our time wondering if it's really possible that you are truly this agreeable. We no longer feel challenged so we try to test the boundaries. We say whatever we want, whenever we want. And it's always just fine with you. We know the Yes Girl well and she's great early in the relationship, but in the end, an independent woman is so much more fun, sexy, and exciting to be with than the "agree with everything" type. Because we *shouldn't* be allowed to get away with everything or to always get our way.

Reason #2: You don't bring a lot to the table.

Relationships are about give and take. But you wouldn't know it if you were involved with a Yes Girl. Although it seems like Yes Girl is a giver—and she'll be the first one to say that she puts other people's needs ahead of her own—she actually ends up doing most of the taking.

Ask any guy who has ever dated you what you taught him or what you brought to the relationship and he will likely be stumped for an answer. Instead, what he'll remember is how he continued his life just as if nothing changed, while you pitched in playing cheerleader and constant companion. He won't think, *Oh, that's right, before Yes Girl, I had no idea about the wonders of classical music, Woody Allen movies, or the men's department at Bloomingdale's.* Nope, he'll be thinking, *Well, she learned how to build a fire, fix a leaky faucet, and interpret batting averages. I was such a positive force in her life. Hmmm . . . I hope she's doing all right without me.*

I know it may not always seem like it when we're bending over backward trying to impress you with all our worldly knowledge, but we want to learn too. Really, we do. So show us what you like. Wear down our resistance. Force feed it to us if you have to. Take us out to sushi. Make us use chopsticks. Every now and then, go ahead and buy us tickets for the musical you've been dying to see. Go ahead and buy that red wine for dinner even though you know we typically prefer beer. Ultimately, we admire the fact that you are broadening our horizons and we're not so stupid that we don't realize variety is the spice of life. After your efforts, if we still don't get it, fine. But at least no one will say that you never tried. And I guarantee we will respect you for attempting to introduce us to something new—even if outwardly we are bitching and moaning. (Just don't plan one of your special evenings on the same night as the big game!)

The Dead Giveaways

The first few times a guy heads out with a Yes Girl, he may not even realize what's happening. You're hanging on to our every word, asking us detailed questions, making meaningful eye contact, and nodding your head knowingly. You seem to really care about what we have to say.

Then we start talking trash. But you just keep on nodding. It's called Yes Girl on autopilot and it's one of the ways guys figure out whether you're really in sync or just trying to feed us a line. We're spouting nonsense and waiting for you to call us out. When that doesn't happen, it dawns on us: You're a Yes Girl.

Busted.

Dead Giveaway #1: I don't know. What do you want to do?
"I can't tell you how many times I've been on the phone trying to make plans with a woman, and it's like she moved to the city yesterday. Half the time, they have no ideas. It's not that I can't take charge, but sometimes it's just nice to know that we're on the same page as far as what we consider to be fun. I cringe every time I hear a woman say, 'I don't know. What do you want to do?'"
—Daniel, 28, Boulder, CO

We've all spent more than enough of our lives playing the "what do you want to do" game. Depending on how fearful you and your date are of hazarding a preference, this back-and-forth can go on indefinitely. Let me suggest that the next time someone asks what you want to do, you have a good answer. Think about it in advance if you have to—just have a plan ready to go.

Coming up with a decent date idea will involve some work on your part. You may have to read up on the new restaurants or think back to all the places where you've already dined to figure out which are your favorites. If you have never thought to do this before, you are in luck. Right here and now is where you start putting an end to your days as a Yes Girl. Use the space below to make a list of your five favorite restaurants:

1. _____
2. _____
3. _____
4. _____
5. _____

Dead Giveaway #2: You let us slide

"A few nights ago, my boyfriend told me that he was too tired to do anything and would just stay in all night. But the other day, we were on the phone and he let slip that he went to a party with his friends that night. I didn't say anything, but the conversation became awkward and tense. I'm getting the feeling I may be losing him."
—Susan, 24, Cedar Rapids, IA

Susan, I hate to pour lemon juice all over your paper cut, but I'm going to tell you what you already know: You have got to stand up for yourself. Your fear of confrontation has been allowed to grow for far too long. When it gets to the point that you can't even tell your boyfriend that you've caught him red-handed in an outright lie, you know the situation is pretty dire.

The worst part is that by avoiding all arguments, Susan is just letting her boyfriend know that he can do whatever he pleases, even hurt her, with no consequences. Her first mistake is thinking that her boyfriend didn't realize he slipped up. Her second mistake is thinking he didn't realize that she chickened out of calling him on it. Her last and most crucial mistake is believing that being in an unfulfilling relationship is better than winding up alone after a relationship-ending argument.

The Unfortunate Side of Saying Yes

Being perfect has a price. Unfortunately, it's the people who try the hardest to please others that end up having to pay it. That's right, Yes Girl, I'm talking to you. Working overtime to make sure everyone else is happy will not only ensure that people take you for granted, but over time it can actually be hazardous to your health.

Living up to the expectations of others instead of setting your own priorities causes resentment to build up. No matter how much respect you may get from others, it cannot make up for the respect you fail to extend to yourself every time you overlook your own needs to make someone else happy.

Admit it—you often feel people are nothing if not ungrateful. That kind of suppressed anger can take a toll in the form of depression, compulsive behaviors, sleep disorders, eating disorders, and a compromised immune system. The list goes on and on. I know how hard it is to separate what you want from what society expects. You don't just magically figure it out overnight. Still, if you want a happy life and a truly satisfying relationship, you're going to have to start the process and learn when to put yourself first. You need to discover yourself and define who you are, *before* you allow yourself to become defined solely by your relationship.

WHAT HAPPENS AFTER HE LEAVES?

If you are defined only by the man in your life, what are you left with when he leaves? Bitterness? Disappointment? How about a lack of identity? All of those things for certain, but worst of all, you will always have the inevitable question of "Why?" It makes no sense to the Yes Girl that her boyfriend would seek greener pastures. After all, she has given him *everything*. Why would he leave? Why? Why?

Yes, the Yes Girl is left with a broken heart and a lot of confusion. And it's not the kind of temporary grief that the rest of us feel after a painful breakup. It's a deep-seated sadness that results from looking in the mirror and realizing that your entire definition of self is gone. All of your friends were his friends. All of your hobbies were his hobbies. You very easily fall into depression because not only has he gone, but it's as if he's taken everything with him and you are left with nothing.

So what do you do? You go through the post-breakup months blaming your ex-boyfriend for being such an idiot. Your friends that still remain, in their attempt to be supportive, confirm your assumption that he is a complete asshole. "It's him, not you."

How could he let go of someone who was so self-sacrificing and so nice to him? Well, the answer is not an easy one. I'm sure he thought long and hard about the decision, because at the end of the day, we do recognize how well you treat us. We do care about you. We do realize that you are a great person. But . . . with no passion, challenge, or excitement in the relationship, we are forced to say good-bye—a decision that's all the more difficult because we realize how much it is going to hurt you.

Don't Date That Guy

As promised, I'm now going to tell you about the guys you can expect to attract if you don't put the brakes on the whole Yes Girl bit. You may be excellent at attracting great guys on a temporary basis, but you're really going to struggle in the long-term relationship bliss category if you don't start making some behavioral changes. Trust me, the kind of man you want wouldn't be caught dead rounding the one-year anniversary corner with a woman who added about as much to the relationship as one of those inflatable girlfriends-in-a-box. However, one of these three big egos just might be more tolerant:

- **Mr. "Me Me Me" Guy:** This guy may seem perfectly normal at first, but at heart, he really only cares about himself. Completely self-absorbed, he sincerely believes that if he's happy, everybody else should be as well. You two will get along great because the more you agree with him, the smarter he will think you are.

- **Mr. Macho Guy:** Here's a man who thinks that his woman should go wherever he goes. If you start expressing some individuality, say, by declining to join him on a leisurely stroll during an arctic freeze, he will feel hurt and possibly angry. And if you start disagreeing too much, that will spell the end of the affair.

- **Mr. "Don't Worry Your Pretty Little Head" Guy:** The Yes Girl's dependent and insecure nature may lead her straight into the evil clutches of this controlling "trophy girl" hunter. He may have money to spend or claim to know what's best for you, but don't confuse his gifts for generosity or his tendency to take over every aspect of your life for kindness. Once he wins you over, he will expect to have all the power in the relationship. This relationship is bound to end abruptly as soon as you learn how to say no.

Three Cheers for You

For all the good you try to do, there just doesn't seem to be enough appreciation wafting in your general direction. Sure, people may nod their heads at the mention of your name and say, "Sue? Oh yeah, she's a great girl." But for some reason it's the squeaky wheels, the ones who ask for what they want and complain when they're dissatisfied, who always seem to get the most consideration. And now I'm adding to the general lack of appreciation in your life with this chapter and all the abuse it has heaped upon you! But the truth is, Yes Girls have a lot of wonderful, desirable qualities. To name a few, you:

- **Strive for perfection:** When you do something, you want to do it right. You hold yourself up to a high standard and will go to great lengths to achieve success. You've just been slightly misguided in your attempts to achieve success in your relationships.
- **Considerate of others:** Your ability to put others ahead of yourself means that you are intensely tuned in to the moods and needs of other people. This is an amazing quality that will serve you better once you learn to tune in to yourself as well.
- **Nurturing:** The desire to take care of other people and make them feel good is an enviable trait. While caretaking likely comes naturally to you, do not underestimate this wonderful quality. You are a nice person, so don't condemn yourself for it!
- **Helpful:** If a friend in need is a friend in deed, you are a real friend. You might not be charming people with your elusive, hard-to-get ways, but you're definitely someone to rely on when the going gets tough.

Your Rx: Go Through a Selfish Phase

Your incessant worrying about what other people will think and feel has gone on far too long. You've served your time and you've earned the right to do whatever makes you happy. Of course, you may have to figure out what that is first. That's what the selfish phase is all about—discovering what you like and then doing it by . . .

1. **Getting out of your comfort zone.** Let this be a challenge to you—take one week to think differently. Start getting out of your comfort zone by making small changes and upending your own habits. Wake up fifteen minutes earlier each day and spend that time doing something you enjoy. Walk a different route to work every day of the week. Eat lunch at a different restaurant every day of the week. Set aside one day of the week-end to act as your own camp counselor. Pretend you're trying to show yourself a good time in your city, create an itinerary, and follow it! You'll find yourself opening up to new and exciting opportunities and having more interesting tales to relay at the dinner table than you've ever had before. And you'll never get stuck in that "I don't know, what do you want to do?" rut ever again.

2. **Assertiveness Training:** If you're realizing that you are something of a Yes Girl, start focusing on putting yourself first. You've been discounting your own needs for so long that you'll have to go to the opposite extreme to correct the imbalance. So start giving yourself the same consideration you would give to the most important person in your life. When you feel tired, stay in—even if you may disappoint people. If you think you've been wronged, say so—even if the slight is something minor. Should all this prove difficult, enroll in some sort of course that will

teach you how to stand up for yourself, such as a self-defense class or a course on management.

3. Pump Yourself Up: To develop a stronger personality you may want to develop a stronger body. There's nothing like a good workout or run to speed up your heart rate, increase your energy, and generally give you a feeling that you can take on the world and win. The stronger you feel, the bolder you'll be.

In the end, you'll know you've come full circle when you have no problem saying no whenever you feel like it—whether at work, to your friends, or to your significant other. Eventually you'll find the right balance between saying no and saying yes.

Fake It Till You Make It

If, every time you get involved with a new guy, all your friends roll their eyes as if to say "see you when you get out in three-to-six months," it's time to at least start *pretending* that you have a life of your own and that you actually care enough to keep it. Here are a few surefire ways to do just that:

- **Say when:** I know you usually just hang out with your boyfriend until he says he's got a lot to do. I want you to try something different. From now on, make sure you are the one who cuts your time together short. Say you've got errands to run and skedaddle. Better yet, take up a new hobby that has nothing to do with him and go do it!
- **Start a turf war:** He wants you over at his place all the time. And so far, he's had his way. Well, today is where that ends. Unless you have some truly awful

roommate situation, you insist that he make his way over to your part of town. If he doesn't come, don't give in. See what happens.

- **Talk about yourself:** All his yarns may not be spun of gold, yet you still hear him out. So what if what you did that day isn't particularly fascinating? You need to practice putting yourself first, so make him sit through a rendition of how you went to the gym, argued with the cabdriver, and barely made it to work on time.

- **Play devil's advocate:** Begin a conversation about something controversial and disagree with his position. Playing devil's advocate in conversation is much more stimulating than always agreeing.

- **Refuse a favor:** Now this advice goes for friends as well as love interests. Next time a friend, boyfriend, relative, or general acquaintance asks you to take time out of your day to do them a favor, just say no if it doesn't work well with your schedule. Yes, you'll be racked with guilt the first time you try it, but if you sugarcoat your "no" with a whole lot of sweet "I'm so sorry" and "You know I love you, buts" you'll find that it's quite liberating to keep your friends while doing just as you wish.

- **Plan a date:** If you are starting to realize that you are a Yes Girl in your relationship, surprise your boyfriend with some spontaneity. Pick one of those favorite restaurants you listed earlier and plan a night out on the town. Tell your boyfriend to wear some nice clothes and that the evening is going to be a surprise. If he complains all night, that could be your first indication that you may be better off without him. (Of course, you need to give him a few more chances before you kick him to the curb.) But, if he enjoys it, well then, you've officially established yourself as an independent woman in the relationship. Any self-respecting man will embrace your newfound boldness in making decisions and plans.

Drama Queen Girl

After an all-night shift in the ER, I sometimes fall asleep in front of the TV and wake up to a daytime soap opera. Talk about your drama queens! The Drama Queen Girl seems to think that all the world's an *All My Children* soundstage. She won't think twice about taking up three hours of her friend's life to discuss her last date. She will devote four or five pages of prime personal journal real estate to the cute guy who smiled at her earlier that day. She can spend hours working to ensure that her text message to a guy she just met is a perfect blend of cute and funny (and she has no problem sending said text to her five closest friends for review before she finally dispatches it to him). She is the woman whose way of saying hello to her dates, pals, and coworkers is "Ohmigod! Have I got a story for you!" She also can't seem to have one glass of wine without dissolving into sobs and sniffles over the great love of her life, the one who got away . . . five years ago.

In short, she's the girl who you just want to shake some sense into. She's the one who makes you want to say, "Would you chill out!," "It's no big deal!," or "Get over it, already!" Of course, if you did that, she'd probably come back with, "Well, you just don't understand. Obviously, you've never felt what I am feeling." Then again, she may be the one whose messy train wreck of a life you love to discuss with your friends. She certainly makes most of us look like we've got it together. Or, perhaps, you don't know any Drama Queen Girls, because there's only room for one Drama Queen in anyone's life and, guess what? Maybe you are her.

I Used to Be That Girl: Jane's Story

"I used to be a terror. And I had no clue. I always blamed other people. If my coworkers didn't take to me, well, they were just jealous. If a guy didn't ask me out for a second date, well, he was just a jerk. There was always a reason for why I was unhappy and it never had anything to do with me. One day, I was complaining about someone to my friend, and she said simply, 'It's not always other people, Jane.' That clicked for me. I thought, *If it's not always other people, then sometimes it must be me.* I guess that's what you'd call my *Oprah* A-ha moment. After that I started making changes."
—Jane, 28, Sociology Grad Student

The Drama Queen thrives on conflict, passion, excitement, adventure. If she's not experiencing some form of anxiety, she's at a complete loss for what to talk about. Since she lives for attention, being quiet is simply not in her playbook. That would mean letting someone else have center stage and actually having to listen. Can you say . . . zzzz . . . zzzz . . . zzzz? And since in this Drama Queen's mind, listening is not only a bore but tantamount to playing second fiddle, she will do whatever it takes to stay in the limelight. And by whatever it takes, I mean just that—from drunken screaming matches at the bar to suicidal gestures, Drama Queen Girl will use every device in her arsenal to get attention.

The truth is, there's a big difference between big-talking, swaggering bravado and genuine confidence. *That* girl, in this case the Drama Queen, is all talk. She can go on all day about how great she is, but anyone with any sense can see that if she really believed in herself, she wouldn't need to.

Could You Be Addicted to Drama?

Tempestuous love affairs, ugly breakups, sorrows drowned in tequila bottles, and reckless behavior tend to follow the Drama Queen Girl around. If that sounds familiar, answer the following questions to find out whether the rest of this chapter is all about you as well:

1. **T / F**   I often exaggerate when telling a story so people give it the attention it deserves.

2. **T / F**   Most of my conversations revolve around the latest catastrophe to befall me.

3. **T / F**   Arguments are crucial in a relationship. If there is no conflict, not only am I bored to death, but I don't have anything to discuss with my friends later.

4. **T / F**   If it's a choice between the heart and the head, I'll follow my heart.

5. **T / F**   I've cried at work many times.

6. **T / F**   I am the life of the party and the most fun to be around.

7. **T / F**   People who criticize me are usually just jealous.

8. **T / F**   I am no stranger to yelling and screaming to get my way or to express my dissatisfaction.

9. **T / F**   I have had a much harder life than most people realize.

10.   **T / F** Usually, I'm the one who is calling my friends. I know they want to talk to me and am sure they'd call me if they had anything to say. They just don't have as much going on as I do.

Scoring:

0-2 True: Sure you have your Paris Hilton moments, but that's probably more due to PMS than a Drama Queen Girl personality disorder.

3-5 True: Uh-oh . . . looks like we have a problem. You are something of a Drama Queen Girl. The fact that it could be a lot worse isn't to say that it can't be a lot better. So read on.

6+ True: You are such a Drama Queen that you're occasionally even annoyed with yourself. Oh, you're not? Well, let me assure you that everyone around you is. Before you turn the rest of the world against you, read this chapter. You of all people can really use a little self-awareness.

Two Reasons Why Guys Don't Like Drama Queens

As a certifiable Drama Queen, you probably think you are perfect just the way you are. You may even think that your worst flaws and drawbacks somehow contribute to your unique, individual charm. Well, here's a newsflash for you: YOU ARE THE ONLY ONE WHO FEELS THIS WAY. Maybe deep down you know this, or maybe you don't. Either way, it's time to ditch the dramatic funk that has defined your life.

Since you probably value your opinion above all others, you may be tempted to chalk up what I'm saying to jealousy or sour grapes. You may even do what so many Drama Queens do and blame me for your problems. As in, *What does he know? He's just calling me a Drama Queen because he can't get an exciting, vivacious woman such as myself to go out with him. Or, Drama Queen? Ha! Doesn't he mean too much woman for him?*

Yes, I know how you Drama Queens think . . . but if it hasn't gotten you discovered by the man of your dreams thus far, the chances of your shtick getting you anywhere in the future are slim. So let's take a moment to understand why any normal, well-adjusted male would run for his life when being chased by a Drama Queen.

Reason #1: You let us down.

One of the most important lessons I've learned in my life is to manage expectations. In other words, if you over-promise and under-deliver, you will disappoint people and they will grow to dislike you.

Unfortunately, Drama Queen Girls don't want to grow on people. You want instant gratification and immediate love. Great at first impressions and awful at follow-through, you blow into our lives full of energy and excitement. By the time your opening act is over, everyone wants to be your friend. But cut to two weeks later and people are rolling their eyes at the mere mention of Ms. Drama Queen's name. It never fails—there's just not enough substance to back up all the expectations you set up with your emotional, flashy style.

The thing about Drama Queens is that they leave no place for the relationship to go. They'll tell you their life story and pour their hearts out in the first few hours of getting to know you. But after the initial rush of that fast connection, it's all downhill. Since you can't possibly be expected to keep up the same level of intensity over time, the relationship quickly becomes mundane and fizzles out.

Reason #2: You wear us out.

Most of the time, the Drama Queen doesn't become boring because she stops being dramatic, she becomes boring because her act gets old. And the poor guy she's dating, aka her audience, gets tired. Tired of listening to stories about her evil parents. Tired of hearing about the latest arguments with her best friends. Tired of listening to complaints about how everyone at work is out to get her. Tired of hearing about her latest plot to rule the world. Tired of hearing and listening, period. Hey, sometimes we'd like to get a word in edgewise and actually believe you are tuning in to us!

Most of all, though, we get tired of the drama you create in the relationship. With a Drama Queen, a guy always feels like he's walking on eggshells. Anything we say and do can be used against us. In a Drama Queen's life, even an innocent comment can be misconstrued into an insult. If I tell you that I like your new hairstyle, you'll probably pout and sulk because you'll take it to mean that I hated how your hair used to look. If I listen to you complain for an hour and then have to leave to meet some friends, I get called out for not being supportive. Everything is an argument—talk about exhausting!

Anyone involved with you Drama Queens knows that it's all work and no play. So while you're strutting around thinking you're being fascinating, fun, and the furthest thing from boring, the rest of us are usually just looking for our chance to get off the phone, out of the room, or away from the relationship.

TEN REASONS TO RELAX—AND BE HAPPY.

We all know people who seem to think that being (or even just seeming) perpetually tormented and self-absorbed is somehow cool. People who actually seem to work at being unhappy. I don't know about you, but I respond much better to a warm smile, an easy laugh, and a happy disposition. If you need actual, concrete reasons to strive for happiness and drop the Drama Queen act, here are several. Happy women are more likely to:

1. Be promoted at work
2. Be considered attractive
3. Earn more money
4. Be approached and pursued by men
5. Enjoy fulfilling marriages
6. Have good luck
7. Live longer, healthier lives
8. Have more friends
9. Be close with their families
10. Get what they want

And that's not just my humble opinion. In 2005, a University of California, Riverside study found that it is happiness and not just hard work that generates both personal and professional success. What's more, they found that it's not success that brings about happiness, but the other way around! So if you're creating drama that produces negativity in your life, stop. Put a smile on your face and focus on the positive, and pretty soon you won't have to construct elaborate tales or engage in outrageous behavior to get people's attention.

The Dead Giveaways

Where to start? Most dramatic women may as well have the words "Drama Queen" tattooed on their forehead for all the subtlety of their presentation. Run-on sentences, volatile mood swings, and irrational behavior are just a few hallmarks of Ms. Dramarama.

If you fall into this category, maybe you've just recently fallen into this self-absorbed pattern because you're only now learning to get in touch with the emotions you would have been better off getting a grip on back in high school when they were more age-appropriate. Or maybe you're a confirmed Drama Queen who hasn't relinquished the throne in years, simply refusing to take responsibility for your behavior and move on with your life as a stable adult. Either way, you're screwing up your relationships. I promise you that while your friends may tolerate your behavior, laugh at your mishaps, and even pretend to care about your stories, guys will stop thinking of you as someone with serious relationship potential as soon as they catch on to your game.

Dead Giveaway #1: Too Much, Too Soon

"I met Paul at a friend's party and we had immediate chemistry. We talked and made out all night and he called me the following day. It was a true cosmic connection. I was completely head-over-heels in love with him. I was sure that this was the real thing. Then he just stopped calling me. This after we'd shared some of the most intimate details of our lives, and after I told him I loved him. What's wrong with men?"
—Liz, 33, Los Angeles, CA

I know what you think I'm about to say. But I'm not going to do it. No way. I am absolutely not going to tell you that it is a terrible, horrible, god-awful misguided idea to tell a man for whom you have intense feelings—and who obviously feels the same way, because, let's face it, you wouldn't be feeling so much if he wasn't feeling the same thing, right?—that you are in love with him after just a few conversations. That would be stating the obvious, and that's not what this book is about.

What I will tell you instead is that if you are a Drama Queen, not only are you highly likely to act on your emotions, but you are even more likely to overreact. And that scares people!

The thing about relationships is that they work best when two people are on the same page—thus the word "connection." As a Drama Queen Girl, you have a tendency to act on impulse and without consideration for the feelings of your love interest. Once you do that, the consequences for the relationship can be disastrous. Whether you get angry enough to tell someone that you hate everything about him or get so amorous as to reveal your love too soon in the relationship, you run the risk of spooking your guy straight into the arms of a calmer, more self-assured woman.

Dead Giveaway #2: Never Happy

"Last week, I went out with a man I'd been seeing for a few weeks. The restaurant he chose looked fine at first, but then we had to wait twenty minutes for a table. And when they finally sat us, we were way in the back and the food was just so-so. After dinner, we went to a comedy club. The comedians weren't funny at all, and I wouldn't even dress my shih tzu in some of the things that audience members were wearing. And I said as much to my date. If you have nothing nice to say, come sit by me. That's my motto."
—Maddy, 36, Chicago, IL

Take a minute to picture the adolescents who are riding puberty's hormonal roller coaster. As you may have noticed, they think it's totally cool to be a little bit annoyed and more than a little bit snotty all the time. Now, give those kids a professional blow-out, put them in some stilettos and a coat of red lipstick, and you're going to have a hard time telling them apart from someone like

Maddy, who is clearly a full-fledged, card-carrying member of the Drama Queen Club.

Whiny, surly, and rarely satisfied, drama queens elevate complaining into an art form. I hate to be the one to break this to you, but while you may believe that all this angst combines to make you one tough cookie and a truly fascinating person to be around, you're a lot less interesting than you think.

You may have learned it in junior high school, or from watching one too many teen movies, but somewhere along the way you got the impression that a happy disposition is boring, conformist, and downright fake, while a bad attitude is a sure sign of individuality, intelligence, and coolness. If that sounds about right, keep reading, because you are in desperate need of a reality check.

The truth is, while Hollywood scripts need constant conflict to stay interesting, most healthy, non-drama-addicted people prefer laughter, harmony, and tranquility to anger, tension, and confrontation. So those of us who stopped confusing whining and put-downs for conversation back in high school will stay far away from you, because it's obvious that you're stuck in that ridiculous drama place, and are just not that much fun to be around for those of us who have long since moved on.

GET A GRIP!

For most of us, it's easy to be positive in familiar or comfortable situations. Unfortunately, when we experience stress—say your date cancels *after* you've already gotten all dressed up, or you're running late and the cashier is taking forever—some people simply lose their cool. And since Drama Queens are by nature high-maintenance, they are likely to freak out quickly when something goes wrong. Need an example of why you should never lose your cool? A very good friend of mine recently went out on a group date with a woman who actually stood up and yelled at him in front of an entire restaurant because she felt he was not paying enough attention to her. Never mind that he was just engaging in conversation with some good friends that he had not seen in a very long time. After screaming at him, she stormed out of the restaurant. Fifteen minutes later, she returned, crying and telling him that she wanted "to make this work." That was their second date, and, despite his attraction to her, he had to make that date their last.

There are always going to be times when you feel like you just want to snap someone's head off, but that's when keeping a positive attitude is even more important. I know what you may be thinking: "Ha! Easy for you to have a good attitude, Doctor Bachelor. But some of us have real problems. My parents don't understand me. I owe more money than I can make in a year. I can't seem to kick my addiction to Krispy Kreme. And on top of all that, I am bored out of my mind in this podunk town!"

"I'm entitled to be negative/angry/moody/depressed" is the single most common argument coming from those who have succumbed to a bad attitude. But I know firsthand that circumstances don't dictate attitude. I'm sure you can imagine how being a doctor has given me the opportunity to meet plenty of people who manage to keep an optimistic outlook despite some of the hardest situations known to humankind. But to stay positive even in the worst times, you have to practice. Try these tips the next time you feel your good attitude slipping away:

1. Think of their families: The next time you hear yourself snapping at a coworker or waiter because they happen to be acting less than perfect on a day when you're feeling less than tolerant, imagine how you would feel if someone spoke to your mother, father, or brother that way? Talk about an instant check to your conscience.

2. Kill them with kindness: When you're dealing with someone negative, don't get mad, get sympathetic. Here is a person who is obviously in pain and clueless about how hard they're making life for themselves, to say nothing of those around them. They deserve your pity, not your retaliation. It's like your mom used to say: "Don't stoop to their level." And "take the high road." And, oh yeah, "be the bigger person." If you don't, you'll just be kicking yourself later for letting someone ruin your mood.

3. Put a smile in your voice: People who smile and laugh frequently are generally perceived as more likeable and positive. When you smile, you're sending a clear message that says, "I mean no harm." If you're on the phone and would like to communicate a friendly attitude to someone who you may not know, keep a smile on your face throughout the conversation.

4. Don't sweat the small stuff: Even if you're stuck in traffic and about to miss the party of the year, you don't have to give in to frustration. Remember, your attitude is up to you to decide. You can choose to work yourself into a frenzy, burst into tears, and beat your fists on the steering wheel, or you can choose to kick back, turn on some great music, sing to your heart's content, and ponder all the reasons why the Universe doesn't want you at that party. If the traffic jam ever does let up, you'll certainly look more presentable and feel more upbeat when you arrive than if you'd gone with the first option.

5. Look for the light: No matter what's going wrong, you can bet that there's always going to be a light at the end of the tunnel.

Dead Giveaway #3: Love Is a Battlefield

"I was involved with Cara for about a year. Although I loved her, in retrospect I don't know how I ever made it that long. Everything was an argument waiting to happen. After only a few weeks together, I began to feel like I was walking in a minefield. One wrong step or word, and bam! I don't appreciate her enough. I don't consider her feelings. I am selfish. I don't love her. I don't know the meaning of the word love. Finally, I couldn't take it anymore. Now I look back with a sigh of relief. I am so happy to be out of that relationship!"
—Jeff, 27, Raleigh, NC

Woe to the poor guy who doesn't pick up on your Drama Queen ways early in the relationship. While many guys figure out what's going on soon enough, some have to suffer a little longer to learn what it is about you Drama Girls that make you so impossible: At heart, you're extremely high-maintenance and don't know how or why to pick your battles.

Admit it. Even the most innocent act or comment can rub you the wrong way. And since you simply refuse to sort through any of your emotions in private or in silence (why bother when it feels so much better to vent?), your long-suffering boyfriends, family, and friends constantly have their hands full.

Men who have had experience with Drama Queens can quickly sniff out what's going on based on your self-centered conversation and your general "God's gift to humankind" persona. If you're not getting what you want, whether it be our attention or our obedience to your whims, man, are we in trouble! And since you're probably not Naomi Campbell and we're probably not your personal assistant, please don't be surprised when we leave before you have the chance to attack us with your cell phone.

THE MANY FACES OF A DRAMA QUEEN GIRL

Drama Queen Girls appear in a wide range of guises. But while each of you goes to extremes in your own special way, the five most popular archetypes are:

1. The Liar: Embellishments, exaggerations, flat-out lies . . . why let a little thing like the truth stand in the way of the love and attention you deserve? If you are this type of Drama Queen, you are an actress in the true sense of the word. You'll actually play-act to get approval.

2. The Psycho: Let me guess. If you fall into this category, you have an "I'm okay, you all suck" attitude. After all, "there's nothing wrong with me, it's the rest of the world that's screwed up." You will get mad at the drop of a hat and cry over spilled milk. Literally. I hate to be the one to break it to you, but you know those whispers and muffled giggles you overhear from your friends and coworkers? They're about you.

3. The Heroine: You may not realize it, but to hear you talk one would think you had just stepped out of the pages of an old-fashioned romance novel. You paint even the briefest fling as the love affair of the century, frequently suggest that you first met your latest boyfriend in a past life, and truly believe that yours are the deepest, most passionate love stories since Romeo and Juliet. You're always suffering for love, and to be honest, people are getting a little tired.

4. The Victim: Poor you. Life has handed you nothing but one terrible hand after another. Your family. Your friends. Your business partners. Your exes. All have proven to be bitter disappointments. The petty jealousies and self-interests of others along with plain old bad luck have made your life so very much harder than anybody else's. And you never miss a chance to inform people of that.

5. The Diva: Not only are you the most deserving person you know, but you are also the most demanding. You have a list of needs that rivals Mariah Carey's backstage rider, and you're ready to fight for every single one of them. Deep down you believe that compromise is for the weak and feel entitled to get whatever you want. Even if that means starting arguments and threatening to walk out on relationships.

The Scary Side of Drama

So far in this chapter, I've stuck to talking about the lighter side of drama. Since the Drama Queen can turn even the most mundane event into a tragedy, she's annoying to be around but usually relatively harmless overall. The thing about drama, however, is that it has a tendency to get out of control and take on a life of its own. And what kind of a doctor would I be if I didn't speak at least a few words of caution?

Every Drama Queen starts out as a Drama Princess. Like the Queen, the Princess is uncomfortable with the humdrum realities of the everyday and dreams of a life a bit less ordinary. She thinks being hyperanimated is more fun for everyone. So she acts out. Exaggerates. Seeks to dominate the spotlight. But it's one thing to blow things slightly out of proportion because you think it makes your stories more exciting, and quite another to get so caught up in your life's events that you lose all perspective, waive *adios* to good reasoning, and become a full-blown Drama Queen, completely driven by your attention-seeking impulses.

As you know only too well, it's not easy being a Drama Queen. Acting on impulse—whether to speak in anger or to buy a big ticket item on a whim—often leaves you feeling guilty and down on yourself. No wonder then that so often it's the Drama Queen Girls who end up in the ER for:

- Drug overdoses
- Drug or alcohol addiction
- Emotional breakdowns
- Suicide attempts

The constant breakups, breakdowns, sob fests, and knock-down-drag-out fights can get to be too much for those who don't learn to effect peace and goodwill. After all, one person can take only so much. But, as the saying goes, while God may not give you more than you can handle, it's easy to get in over your head when you're the architect of your own drama. The fact that a lot of the tragedy is self-created doesn't make it any less real. Spend one night in the ER and you'll know that an overly dramatic life can create some very real problems, including those mentioned above. And although I've intentionally been a bit playful while poking fun at the Drama Queen lifestyle, it's only because I truly believe it is never too late to look in the mirror and make some changes.

Don't Date That Guy

I probably don't have to tell you that at first many men are often impressed and attracted to Drama Queens. Your over-the-top personality can be extremely magnetic and you are very aware that you have mastered the first impression. However, after the initial thrill wears off, you have probably found that most guys set their course for calmer waters. With the exception of the following:

- **Mr. Drama King:** While this guy thinks he's all heart, the rest of the world has pretty much pegged him as a hothead. The Drama King winds up driving you crazy by giving you a taste of your own medicine. He's never met a disagreement he couldn't win, even

if that means arguing about the thermostat for hours.
Now, I know you think you can dish it out, but can
you take it? These relationships tend to go out in a
blaze of glory—to the sound of dishes breaking and
stemware shattering.

- **Mr. Boring Guy:** This guy sees you as the answer
to his prayers. He is so sick and tired of his life, yet
so powerless to make any real changes, that he turns
to you for life support. Unfortunately, if he doesn't
sound like he brings a lot to the table, that's because
he doesn't. You will quickly tire of his agreeable ways
and blind adoration.

Don't Let Me Drum You Out of the Business

I know I've said a lot of discouraging words in this chapter. But
as a natural actress, you have to accept that criticism and rejection
are par for the course. Please take what I say as constructive feedback, not as a reason to pack up your props and costumes and go
home. Not at all. Not with so much talent at your disposal. After
all, we've all been overly dramatic. We've all exaggerated.

While you certainly don't want to be *that* girl—the notorious
Drama Queen who has only to launch into a monologue to get
people reaching for their grain of salt—you should definitely hold
on to the positive aspects of your personality that have contributed
to making you who you are. I know, I know! After reading this
chapter, the last thing you're focused on are your positive attri-
butes, but that doesn't mean you don't have plenty. For instance,
you're . . .

- **Energetic:** Believe me, most people would kill to
have a fraction of your energy and get-up-and-go

verve. You can get excited over just about anything. In fact, many of us don't dislike Drama Queens so much as we get exhausted by them. All I'm saying is, just rein it in a little.

- **Engaging:** There's no denying that people are drawn to you and that you can be a lot of fun to spend time with. You have a great ability to open up to people and get them to reciprocate. Take that engaging personality and combine it with honesty and openness and I guarantee you'll never have any shortage of friends.

- **Passionate:** You have intense emotions and no trouble showing them. People marvel at how excitable you are and how readily you throw yourself into every new romance, work project, or friendship, and secretly wish they could do the same. Within limits, of course.

So there you have it—uncontested proof that Drama Queen Girls are actually wonderful, valuable, and exciting human beings. Think about it. While everyone would like to have a fascinating and adventurous life, you manage to impart a sense of drama to your existence no matter what is or isn't going on. No wonder you're the life of the party! Now if you'd only learn how to wield your powers responsibly, people would appreciate what you have to offer so much more. However, if you continue to act as if it's your world and the rest of us are just squatting in it, you'll wind up with little more to show for your love life than one quickly fizzled romance after another. And I know that's not what you really want.

Your Rx: Get Real!

Drama Queens, if you don't want to be *that* girl anymore, you need to get a life—a *real* life, with real events, that won't inspire you to exaggerate or milk every inconsequential detail for its last ounce of drama. Building this life will take some time, but it's not difficult. You can start by:

- **Volunteering:** What better way to get some perspective on your life than to interact with people who have real problems? You can get a dose of some actual life dramas by volunteering your time at a nursing home, hospital, animal shelter, soup kitchen, or any place else where you think your energy will be felt and appreciated. Focusing on helping other less fortunate people will not only curb your Drama Queen tendencies in the short term, but in the long run, it will help you feel good about yourself and your role in the world so that you won't feel the urge for constant hyperbole.

- **Going on a real adventure:** Go on a trek in Nepal (or simply start hiking the trails at a local park). Get a group of friends together and take a cross-country road trip. Sign up for a weeklong bike tour. Take up competitive tennis. Check out a meditation retreat. Once you start living your life to the fullest, you'll see that you don't have to dominate every conversation with the stories of your many conquests. Your accomplishments will speak for themselves.

More than anything else, your unique experiences, open mind, and sense of purpose will combine to affirm your belief in yourself, and when you believe in yourself, people know. And, more often than not, they stick around to find out why.

Fake It Till You Make It

My goal is to help you become so content and satisfied with yourself and what you've got going for you that you'll be able to stop pretending to be something you're not and create solid relationships based on honesty and mutual respect. From that point on, you'll be able to approach relationships with a clear head and will no longer look to them to fill your life with the adventure it's lacking.

I know it sounds like a tall order, but I promise you, it absolutely can be done.

In the meantime, you can downshift on the drama pronto by incorporating these tips into your social life:

- **Be friendly:** Even if you're on a battery of anti-depressant meds, you can still put your best, most drama-free foot forward when you're meeting people for the first time. Smile warmly, make eye contact, and try to come up with at least one nice thing about the person you just met. If the spirit moves you, feel free to pay them the compliment.
- **You ask the questions:** You've gotten so used to doing all the talking that you've forgotten what it's like to sit back, relax, and let someone else sing for their supper. Next time you're in a conversation, focus on learning about the person you're speaking with instead of telling them about yourself. Steer the conversation toward them with leading, open-ended questions such as: What do you like to do? Where

did you grow up? Then let their answers inspire you to ask even more questions. And most important, actually listen!

- **Guard your privacy:** While I would advise most people to open up a bit more, you, Drama Queen Girl, could actually stand to gain from putting up just a tiny little barrier. Here's a tip: Your first conversation with a new guy may not be the best time to go into detail about the demise of your last relationship or the devastating emotional tailspin that followed.

- **Silence is golden:** Have you ever stopped to think about whether you monopolize conversations? The easiest way to stop is to start paying attention to how much you're allowing other people to speak. If you're finding that you're doing more than 50 percent of the talking, cut all the way back to 30 percent. You can use the listening practice.

- **Take a month off from complaining and telling tall tales.** Fine yourself one dollar every time you catch yourself launching into a litany of your problems or hear yourself exaggerating for effect. Stop the self-aggrandizement and just be yourself. It's so much less exhausting. When you've broken your habit, donate that money to charity.

Bitter Girl

We've all been hurt at some point in our lives. We've all been through bad relationships, awful breakups, and the inevitable lonely nights that follow. We've all spent at least a few hours trying to curse the entire opposite sex into oblivion, and some have even resorted to writing poems about loss, heartbreak, and the cruel nature of love. Now, those of you who have gotten over your frustration and moved on to forge satisfying relationships can relax—I can pretty much guarantee that this chapter is not going to hold a lot of relevance for you.

The rest of you, keep reading. You may very well have something in common with Bitter Girl.

I have to admit, sometimes you can't exactly blame people for feeling bitter. I feel bitter just *watching* some of my friends' relationships unfold. But while anger and bitterness are a normal part of post-traumatic-relationship stress, most people strive to move past these negative and counterproductive emotions. Like I said, we've all been there. The hatred and hostility may last a month, a year, or even longer, but eventually they are replaced by kinder, gentler attitudes.

Then there is Bitter Girl. Bitter Girls are easy to spot. If you can't identify one by the ticked-off look on her face, her defensive stance, or the frequent comparisons she draws between men and farm animals, you'll certainly figure it out when you ask for her phone number and she responds with something to the effect of, "Right! Like you're actually going to call!" And heaven help you if she starts in on her ex-boyfriend or ex-husband. To hear her talk about that #$%!, as she still so lovingly calls him, you'd think he got her pregnant, left her at the altar, and ran off with her TV set—and her sister.

But who knows? Maybe he has. That's the sad truth behind the Bitter Girl's tough, take-no-prisoners facade—she is traumatized by her past relationships, and she's hung on to that anger and resentment for so long that they have come to define her entire personality. Any guy who tries to date her will have his work cut out for him, believe me. Deep down, the only thing this woman really wants is revenge, and she will make every man pay for the mistakes of the man who has hurt her.

Oftentimes, Bitter Girls give off a vibe that most men can instantly recognize. She may be the girl who walks into a bar with her nose in the air, looking down just long enough to dismiss the clueless guy who had the poor sense to approach her. Or, more likely, she may be the girl who is never approached while her less-jaded girlfriends get all the attention. Although common sense would dictate that Bitter Girl change her behavior to make a more outgoing and friendly impression, she actually does the opposite, getting even angrier at men and acting out in increasingly hostile ways.

We can also talk about a different type of Bitter Girl, the kind who has tamed the outward signs of bitterness, but subconsciously she still doesn't trust any man enough to let him get too close to her. Since she truly believes that it's only a matter of time before a man disappoints her, she winds up fulfilling her own prophecy by pushing away every guy the moment she begins to feel something for him. Yes, there may be many faces to a Bitter Girl, but they all have one thing in common: They distrust men.

Could you be a Bitter Girl?

If this sounds something like you, but you're still not sure whether or not you fit the bill, take this quiz to find out once and for all.

1. **T / F**   In conversation, I often say that men are jerks.
2. **T / F**   I know it's not PC, but I secretly hope my ex dies alone. Soon.
3. **T / F**   When I start talking about the good-for-nothing dirtbags I once called "significant" others, it's hard for me to stop.
4. **T / F**   I enjoy dumping guys. Better them than me!
5. **T / F**   If there are any good ones, they are either married or taken.
6. **T / F**   I can't imagine being in a happy relationship.
7. **T / F**   True love is an illusion. There's no such thing.
8. **T / F**   Men usually perceive me as bitchy.
9. **T / F**   I have been avoiding relationships because they never work out and someone always gets hurt.
10. **T / F**   It never fails; guys disappear the second they realize that you care.

Scoring:
0-2 True: You are a sweetheart. Sure, you have some doubts about relationships and finding the right guy, but you always manage to keep your heart open.

3-5 True: No two ways about it, you're pretty bitter. But all is not lost. Save yourself by paying close attention to this chapter and taking its advice to heart.

6+ True: If I was a gambling man, I would bet that you will end up way more miserable than any of those horrible exes whose car tires you've slashed with your handy dandy box cutter. Changing your attitude is one of the most difficult challenges anyone can undertake, but I can say with 100 percent certainty that it is completely doable. And I swear to you, if you succeed, you will be happier than you've ever dreamed possible.

Two Reasons Why Guys Don't Like Bitter Girls

Like I alluded to before, there are really two types of Bitter Girls: the brazen Bitter Girl who scowls at everything with facial hair, and the closeted Bitter Girl who is good at hiding her resentment. If you're the former, you probably don't need me to tell you that guys cut a pretty wide swath around you. I know you probably have yourself pretty well convinced that you couldn't care less what these stupid guys think, but underneath all that big talk and swagger, you know you're kidding yourself. If anything, you care too much.

Now, if you're more of a secretly Bitter Girl, you probably go on a fair share of dates and may even get involved in some short-lived relationships. Still, you're no better off than the brazenly Bitter Girl, because all your encounters tend to go nowhere and you wind up alone. Here's why:

Reason #1: We Like to Feel Good.

Here's a tip: People like people who make them feel good. Bitter Girls make us feel terrible. As in awkward. Uncomfortable. Unwanted. Take your pick. Whether we recognize you as bitter right away or when you start pushing us away a bit later in the relationship, the end result is still the same—we suddenly feel like we're about to get rejected.

Here's how it generally plays out: A guy meets Bitter Girl at a party or a bar and starts trying to make friendly conversation. Judging by the look on her face and her general posture, you would think he was begging for cab fare. Not only does she completely shut down, but she seems to go on the offensive. And it's not just that this guy isn't good-looking enough or charming enough or smart enough. The truth is he may very well be the greatest guy in the room, but when Bitter Girl looks at him, all she sees is someone she can't trust. And since she's pretty much figured out that all men are jerks, she's not going to give him the time of day.

The guy will sense this attitude within a few minutes, if not a few seconds, and make himself scarce. Can you blame him? I mean, talk about barking up the wrong tree. The only vibes he's picking up are either coldness or animosity. Meanwhile, his hasty retreat will serve only to further convince Bitter Girl that all guys are rude, obnoxious, and, maybe more to the point, clearly not attracted to her. So she'll become even more embittered. It's a vicious, self-perpetuating cycle. But make no mistake—if you're a Bitter Girl, you're the one who keeps it going.

Reason #2: You Don't Trust Us.

Trust is a crucial component of any good relationship. If I tell you I like you or enjoy spending time with you or any variation on the "I have feelings for you" theme, and your reaction is to think that I don't really mean it or that I am just saying it to get something from you or that I will change my mind as soon as I realize you like me back, well, then we've got a serious problem. It's exhausting having to prove myself all the time.

Bitter Girls with trust issues usually end up putting guys

through endless rounds of tests. Inevitably, the guy is bound to fail one and prove to the Bitter Girl that she was right all along. Relationships never work out for her. All men really *are* jerks. If you fall into this mindset, my guess is that while you want to be with someone, you honestly believe that if you let yourself feel something, you are just going to wind up getting hurt. So instead, you end up pushing guys away.

Just imagine how this must look to the poor guy who is trying to get closer to you. No matter how much you want him to be a mind reader, he's only human. As such, when you start to push him away by either acting evasive or picking arguments, he'll probably jump to the very natural conclusion that you are not that interested in maintaining a relationship with him. Like I said, we can't read your mind. If you act like you'd rather be alone, we will lose faith in you and the relationship. I don't care how evolved a guy may be, patience has its limits and Bitter Girls test these to the breakup point.

WHY DON'T GOOD THINGS HAPPEN TO BITTER PEOPLE?

Allow me to illustrate. Here is how one woman might handle a conversation at a nightclub if she came in with Bitter Girl's negative "I'm okay, you all suck" brand of attitude:

> Random Guy: Hi, how are you?
> Bitter Girl (looking suspicious): Okay.
> Random Guy: You should smile more.
> Bitter Girl: Whatever, weirdo.

Now here is how the conversation could have played out if the same woman had just lightened up for the night and decided not to take it all so seriously:

Random Guy: Hi, how are you?

Fun Girl: Great. You?

Random Guy: We are actually having an awesome night—we're celebrating my best friend's birthday. See the guy over there on the dance floor looking silly? That's him!

Fun Girl: He's just over there proving to the world that most men have no rhythm!

Random Guy: By the way, in a little while we're going to Diddy's party, want to come?

Fun Girl: Sounds like fun. Let me introduce you to some of my friends.

You get the gist. Positive attitudes open doors. Negative attitudes get them slammed in your face. Any questions?

The Dead Giveaways

If I know anything about how you Bitter Girls operate, then you're probably reading this right now and thinking, *Okay, so maybe I am bitter. But it's not as if anyone else can tell, so it can't be the real reason I'm alone and lonely.* That's the ironic thing about Bitter Girls—the reason you are able to reach such extraordinary heights, or should I say lows, of rudeness and offensive behavior is because there's a big part of you that truly believes you're somehow invisible. I don't know how you managed to do it, but if you're a full-blown Bitter Girl, you've probably convinced yourself that it doesn't matter how obnoxious you act toward men, because men are too stupid or disinterested to care or notice.

So, just in case you've been feeding yourself this line of BS, let me take this opportunity to clue you in to how the rest of the world perceives the Bitter Girl.

Dead Giveaway #1: Assuming the worst

"The other night, I went out to some bars with an old friend. She's been divorced for a couple of years and has two beautiful kids. I thought she had it all figured out. I realized that something was way off when she started shooting down any guy who would come up to talk to us. She was so mean to them, too. At many moments, I was truly embarrassed. Worse still, when I met this one guy that I thought was very cute, she suddenly decided it was time to go home. I barely had time to give him my phone number before she pulled me away."
—Robin, 31, New York, NY

If you've ever behaved like Robin's friend, not only are you bitter, but you're showing the world exactly how bitter you are every chance you get. The guys who are approaching you and your friends may not realize what they're up against the second they introduce themselves. But by the time they've shaken your hand, they're picking up on your signal loud and clear. That's why they keep talking to your friend instead of you. It's not necessarily because your friend is prettier, thinner, or carrying a better handbag. It is because she has a more engaging personality. You can quote me on that.

Now I'm not saying you should go out and emulate your more popular girlfriends' personalities. No way. All I'm suggesting is that you take some time to get over your anger long enough to stop jumping to the worst possible conclusions about all men. Sure, some men are jerks and maybe you've been unfortunate enough to have been burned by them on numerous occasions in the past. But if you don't make peace with your past and move on, no man will ever have the chance to prove you wrong.

The reason you're mean to those guys who approach you and your friends isn't because you don't want to talk to any of them. It's because you assume they're approaching for all of the wrong reasons. And who knows? Maybe four out of five times you're right. However, even if only one out of every five guys who comes up to talk to you is legitimately worth your time, if you give him that same evil eye you've been dishing out all night, I can assure you that he's not going to stick around very long. I know I wouldn't.

Dead Giveaway #2: Ranting Mad

"The other night, I went out with a woman I met online. She had great pictures and seemed perfectly normal in her profile. In fact, she seemed perfectly normal most of the evening until she got on the subject of her ex. She didn't say very much, but the little she did say made it clear that she was still extremely angry. It set off some serious warning bells."
—Matt, 26, Seattle, WA

I'm only going to say this once: Nobody who is trying to date you wants to see you get emotional over your ex. On second thought, I'll say it again: No man, woman, or child I have ever met would respond positively to someone who is still either in love with or angry at their ex. If you're no longer hung up on your ex, go ahead and discuss past relationships as much as you want. But if you're still broken up over what happened, avoid the topic like the avian flu. You won't be able to hide your feelings and when your date decides against asking you out again, you will only be left wondering, *Now, why didn't that guy call? We had such a good conversation.*

The only reaction anyone who is interested in you romantically actually wants to see when you talk about past relationships is indifference. Maybe compassion or concern. Certainly not hatred or passion. Women who seem like they want to kill their ex make us fear for our future well-being. So here are your options: You can actually get over the hurts of the past, you can take a break from dating until you're in a better place, or you can "act" as if everything is okay even though you know you're still bitter. I highly recommend against the last option because the only time acting is worthwhile is if you're Jennifer Aniston and get $10 million per movie. Enough said.

The Bitter Pills

I don't want to start wagging my finger at you and telling you about the actual health risks of going through life constantly feeling miserable. I think by now we all know that stress leads to unhealthy habits and high blood pressure, which leads to heart disease, and so forth. I could go on, but I'll stop because the truth is that these physical consequences are nothing compared to the emotional and psychological pain that bitter people put themselves through on a daily basis.

The saddest thing of all about being bitter is that if you spend enough time assuming the worst, eventually you buy into all your own hype and start believing that the world has nothing good in store for you. So you stop taking risks, you don't pursue your dreams, be they personal or professional, and good things actually stop happening to you. Hope is replaced by bitterness, and that's what I call tragic.

Hopefully, you're nowhere near as badly off as all that and I'm getting *way* ahead of the situation. But even if I'm not, and you are as bitter as I just described, read on to find out how to make the kind of meaningful changes that will dramatically improve your life.

Don't Date That Guy

Although your animosity toward men is standing between you and a healthy relationship, it may not keep you from enjoying some very dysfunctional unions. Hard as it may be to believe, there are those guys who are attracted to Bitter Girls. Suffice to say, the following Bitter Girl magnets may have some issues of their own to sort out:

- **Mr. Clueless:** This type of guy is either very naïve or very dumb. He never fails to confuse Bitter Girl's show of bravado for real strength. Oftentimes, he wonders what he could possibly do to be good enough for you. He will try to earn your approval, but you may have a hard time respecting him for his efforts.
- **Mr. Walk All Over Me:** This guy likes to be bossed around. He actually prefers it when you're mean. But while you two might go on to have a perfectly miserable marriage, his friends will always shake their heads as they talk about that awful woman Mr. Walk All Over Me married, and they'll wonder what he could have been thinking.

The Bitter and the Sweet

More than anything else, Bitter Girls deserve compassion. So if after reading this chapter you're starting to realize that maybe you are a Bitter Girl, don't take it too hard. Nobody enters the world feeling bitter. It's a quality people acquire with age, and usually for legitimate reasons. The tragic thing about this type of personality is that it conceals your true nature, which is:

- **Idealistic:** Sadly, bitterness is often the result of disappointed expectations. At one point, you probably thought quite highly of people. It was only when you got hurt that you realized that people, men in particular, are not necessarily looking out for your best interests and that you can't trust everyone. Naturally, you reacted by swinging to the other extreme. But now is the time to return to the center and rediscover the person you really are, a person who is . . .

- **Kind:** The reason you once had such high hopes for the world is because at heart you, yourself, are a very kind person. Certainly it only seemed natural to believe that everyone thought and felt the same way you did. When you realized that this wasn't the case, you decided "no more Miss Nice Girl." And now you're paying the karmic price.

The sweetest and most idealistic people are the ones who can wind up the most embittered. So if you're feeling like your picture should be posted somewhere in this chapter, you're in good company. As a basically decent and righteous person, a little effort is all that stands between you and the light, happy, and warm personality that is your birthright.

Your Rx: Get a New Attitude.

Women like Oprah Winfrey, Katie Couric, and Diane Sawyer may not have much in common when it comes to their looks or lifestyles, but they share a very important characteristic: Famously positive attitudes that make people love them and want to see them every day. Your attitude can do the same for you.

Everyone you come across is personally invested in how you make them feel. Do you get them laughing and feeling at ease with your positive demeanor or are they uncomfortable and anxious to get away? When you've got a good attitude and are generally bringing your best game, you'll attract people with good attitudes who will treat you well. Simply put, behaving like an aloof, unhappy person won't attract the sort of positive, kindhearted person that you ultimately deserve. In fact, you'll probably end up with the kind of jerks you assume that all men are. Take this quiz to find out whether a simple adjustment in your attitude is all it will take to make a world of difference in your life:

Do You Have an Attitude Problem?

Maybe your attitude is just fine as is, then again, maybe not. For all you know, it may be at the root of every problem you've ever spent an afternoon complaining about.

1. You're waiting for an important phone call when you get a call from a telemarketer. You:

   a. Hang up without a word.

   b. Get annoyed and snap at them to put you on the "do not call" list.

   c. Feel bad for the poor telemarketer. What a thankless job! You make an excuse and try not to offend them when you politely ask them to put you on the "do not call" list.

2. You're walking in the park when a bag lady feeding pigeons asks you if you'd like to join her. You:

   a. Hold tight to your handbag and walk by with your head held high.

b. Mumble "no thanks," barely making eye contact.

c. Consider the proposition before either joining in or telling her you'd like to, but are just too rushed at the moment.

3. You and a single girlfriend go to a big launch party. Once you get a chance to sit down, the first thing you talk about is most likely to be:

a. Who's wearing the worst outfit.

b. The absence of really cute guys.

c. Who in the crowd you may want to talk to.

4. When was the last time someone told you that you have a bad attitude?

a. A few weeks ago—or was it just yesterday?—when I yelled at my cab driver for going too slow.

b. Some months back, when my boss was upset that I didn't give her enough notice before going on my vacation, but I'd already confirmed my flight. Like I told her, I'd never get to go on vacation if I had to ask permission three months in advance!

c. In junior high, when I talked back to my substitute teacher.

5. When you are introduced to someone new, either socially or professionally, what is your first thought?

a. Who cares? I'll probably never see this person again.

b. Hmm. I wonder if this person could do anything for me.

c. I don't really think about it. I'm just friendly and let the conversation flow naturally.

Scoring:

Number you answered with *a*: _____ x 1 = _____

Number you answered with *b*: _____ x 2 = _____

Number you answered with *c*: _____ x 3 = _____

Add up your totals in the last column = _____

5–8 points: "Your Own Worst Enemy." All I can guess is that you're ready for a change. You've fallen into a negativity rut—a sinkhole that will drag you down farther and farther if you don't change your ways. Don't worry, I know how you feel. Every time I evaluate an agitated, intoxicated patient in the ER at four in the morning, I fall into my own negativity rut. As I stand at the bedside getting spit on, projectile vomited on, and cursed at, I have to intensely focus on readjusting my less-than-positive attitude every single time. It's not always easy, but it is *always* worth the effort. The key is to be consciously aware of your attitude so you can change it.

9–12 points: "Chip on Your Shoulder." While you are probably getting by okay—neither especially happy nor especially miserable—you deserve a lot more out of life. An attitude adjustment is just the thing to help you get it.

13–15 points: "An All-Around Pleasure." That's what people are saying about you, and you know it.

Don't take your score on this quiz too seriously. It's only meant to be an exercise in self-reflection about how you approach certain situations. But it can help, so keep reading.

Lighten Up! Life's Too Short to Be So Bitter

Your chances of remaining a Bitter Girl are slim if you incorporate the following into your life:

- **An evaluation of how satisfied you are with your job:** It may not even be your exes who are making you bitter, but your job. If you feel unappreciated and uninspired, or dog-tired and overworked, the resulting feelings could be seeping into your personal life, damaging your confidence and marring your overall outlook. If you're unhappy with your job, start looking for other opportunities. Sometimes even just thinking about getting a new job is enough to lighten your spirits.

- **A hobby that you find relaxing and that allows you time to think:** Consider taking up yoga or long-distance running or gardening—anything that helps you to de-stress, feel healthy, and take time for reflection. Then you can unwind and work through your problems rather than just assigning blame.

- **Better eating habits:** Eating healthy is about changing your lifestyle. You've seen what happens to children when they eat too much sugar—a lot of frantic energy, followed by grumpy grogginess. Well, the same happens to adults. It's no wonder you're feeling lethargic, unattractive, and bitter if you're filling up on junk food. Add exercise and see how much better you feel about yourself and how your outlook improves once you start taking care of yourself. Believe me, people will notice the new, more positive you.

YOUR BODY AS A FURNACE

I would not be doing my job as a physician if I didn't at least attempt to take this opportunity to dispel one of the biggest myths about dieting: "the less you eat, the more weight you will lose." While that may be true to some extent, eating less but eating inconsistently can actually cause you to gain weight in the long run. Our bodies need consistent calories as well as exercise to function at a high level.

Those among you who are regular restrictive dieters have

probably tried everything up to and including the Cabbage Soup Diet (don't even get me started on that one!). Some of these diets work for a while, but you know as well as I do that when you crash diet so you can lose five pounds in one week, you're back where you started and looking for a new weight loss regimen come two weeks' time—except now, maybe you've got seven pounds to lose instead of just five.

Think of your body as a furnace and of your metabolism as the fire in that furnace. Your body needs a steady supply of fuel in the form of consistent, healthy calories to keep your furnace running efficiently (and burning calories). That's why it is preferable to eat smaller meals every three to four hours throughout the day, and why withholding food for long stretches can cause weight gain. When you withhold food, your metabolism comes to a grinding halt. Need a visual? Imagine what happens to a fire with no wood. It burns out. The same thing happens to your body's metabolism when you starve your body. You'll feel irritable, lethargic, light-headed, and unmotivated. No wonder studies show that frequent dieters are also the most frequent bingers. Once your furnace, or metabolism, shuts down, you have barely enough energy to sit on the couch with a tub of ice cream. And your body will store those ice cream calories as fat, saving fuel since, if you're eating only sporadically, it's not certain when the next meal is going to come along.

My point is that healthy eating is a lifestyle and *not* a diet. If you want to lose weight, eat healthy meals spread throughout the day and avoid starving yourself. Add exercise and you'll feel even better. Your furnace will thank you. Need ideas for healthy food choices that will keep you satiated throughout the day? Consider subscribing to a magazine like *Cooking Light* or log onto the Internet for healthy recipes. And if you feel yourself getting hungry, eat a healthy snack so your body's metabolism stays in high gear and your furnace burns bright throughout the day.

MY PERSONAL ATTITUDE ADJUSTMENT

Back when I was a resident physician, I worked even crazier hours than I do today. Whenever a week would go by when I wasn't able to get to the gym or go for a run or hike, the same thing would happen: The first few days would be okay, but after five days without any physical activity, I'd feel my energy flag and my spirits sink. My entire outlook on life would change during those weeks when I wasn't able to exercise. I'm a pretty happy-go-lucky person, and what I've come to realize is that I owe a lot of my positive attitude to regular physical activity. Exercise helps relieve the stress in my life.

There are times in the ER when I see things that are so tragic that I feel hopeless and bitter. Engaging in physical activity gives me time to think, and I always end up feeling much better afterward. I put on earphones, crank up my music, and take the opportunity to put life in perspective. Exercise helps me to remain lighthearted when nothing else can. The endorphins really do make a difference. In my opinion, and research supports this, exercise is the all-natural Prozac. The physical benefits are just a bonus.

Fake It Till You Make It

Anger and resentment are deeply seated issues that need to be worked out if you ever expect to have a relationship that isn't stymied by your burning desire to hurt people before they have a chance to hurt you. Here's what you can do right now to stop letting your anger get the best of you and start making a better impression on the people you meet every day:

- **Banish Evil Thoughts:** Oh, we know only too well why you've got that scowl on your face. You're focusing on something negative. Maybe it's the wandering eye of that guy you're talking to, or maybe it's that bad hair day you've been having all week. Whatever the inspiration for your critical internal dialogue, shift gears to something positive, whatever it may be, and use all your mental energy to focus on that.
- **If You Have Nothing Nice to Say . . . :** Next time you're tempted to give someone you've recently met a piece of your mind, take a second to think of him as a person just like you: someone with parents and siblings who love and care about him. Then either say something that will make him feel good, or just keep quiet.
- **Assume the Best:** If someone looks at you, assume it's because they think you're attractive. If someone asks you a question, assume it's because they think you're clever. If someone compliments you, assume those are the truest words they've ever spoken. Do this correctly and the next step will come naturally . . .
- **Smile:** Most people can spot a fake smile, but yours will be genuine once you start relating to the people you're with, focusing on their good qualities, and trusting that they only have the best of intentions. Even if the old adage that it takes forty-three muscles to frown and only seventeen to smile may not be anatomically correct, it sure feels a lot better to smile,

doesn't it? And for those people you meet who *don't* have the best intentions, too bad for them. Just keep smiling and don't let it bother you. They have the problem, not you!

- **Own Your Share of the Blame:** We feel especially bitter when we're blaming other people for our problems. So think back to the last person who hurt you and think about what you may have done to contribute to the situation. Take some time to write down a list of what you did wrong. See? No one is perfect. That's just a fact of life, not a reason to be mad at the world.

Being a Real Friend— Not *THAT* Friend

I am going to tell you a secret: As guys, we are always watching how you treat your friends. In fact, nothing is more concerning than meeting a woman who treats a man like gold but treats her friends poorly. If he's a self-respecting man, it won't take long before he feels like fool's gold and he's out the door.

A couple of weeks ago, my buddy and I had plans to see a basketball game with our friends, Liz, Jessica, and Dana. But when I was with Liz and Jessica a few days before the game, they let me know that they only had four tickets and were planning on telling Dana that the plans were canceled. That bothered me a bit, but I let it go. Then, when we went to the game, the girls went on and on about how Dana is nice, but . . . I could go on, but you get the picture. Dana got stabbed in the back. (The greatest irony is that Dana is the coolest of the bunch.)

I am shocked when I hear women talking behind their friends' backs. This one behavior tells me so much about the woman—and none of it good—that I don't understand how so many women can go around acting as if putting their friends down is not only no big deal, but also somehow cool. The way you treat your friends is a reflection of who you are as a person and how you conduct yourself in every relationship. So you can tell me all about your hatred for small animals or your amazing talent for shoplifting and I'll probably still have a higher opinion of you than if I hear you bad-mouthing the people who are supposed to be your friends.

And it's not just me. Any guy who knows the value of friendship will hear you talking that way and run in the other direction. The untrustworthy, clueless, or like-minded guy may stick around, but come on, is that the kind of guy you want to end up with? Do you want a boyfriend who cheats on you and criticizes you behind your back?

More than anything else, the kind of friend you are tells people what kind of partner you would make in a relationship. The truth is that you can't ever hope to have a solid relationship with a guy until you are able to have good relationships with your friends. After all, the very traits that go into making a woman a great friend—traits like honesty, the ability to communicate, compassion, and loyalty—are the ones that go into making her a fantastic catch in a guy's mind.

So, ask yourself, are you a great friend?

What Kind of Friend Are You?

Some women mistakenly believe that they can be undependable as a friend, but still somehow be a fantastic girlfriend to their significant other. Now, I hate to burst your bubble, but if that's what you think, you're kidding yourself. The way you behave with your girlfriends is inevitably the way you will act with your boyfriend. So take some time to check your friendship skills right here and now:

1. You're on vacation with your friend, who is acting a bit down. When you ask what's wrong, she says she has a sore throat. You:

    a. Think, "Oh no. Not again! Even now she manages to inconvenience me."

    b. Express sympathy, all the while hoping she doesn't bail on your plans.

    c. Realize that she's been pretending to be healthy on your account and send her off to bed while you sightsee on your own for a couple of days.

2. The last time your best friend told you a secret, you:

    a. Told everyone. She never made you pinky-swear!

    b. Only told one other close friend. And that person hardly even knows her, so . . .

    c. Kept it to yourself.

3. Your friend is dating a hottie. At the next dinner party, you:

    a. Flirt a little. It's harmless.

    b. Talk to him and see if he's got a personality to go with those looks.

    c. Talk to him to see what his intentions are in respect to your friend.

4. Your friend calls and tells you she's too exhausted to meet you for dinner. You:

    a. Get really mad. You were counting on getting together and now your night is a bust.

    b. Get annoyed for a minute, but keep it under control. You might have to bail on plans with her in the future.

    c. Take it in stride. You'll either have dinner with another friend or order in. The two of you have plenty of time to catch up later.

5. How would you feel about introducing a new boyfriend to your friends?

a. Embarrassed. My friends don't exactly represent who I am.

b. Apprehensive. I hope they like one another.

c. Proud. I know he'll love them as much as I do.

Scoring:

Number you answered with *a*: _____ x 3 = _____

Number you answered with *b*: _____ x 2 = _____

Number you answered with *c*: _____ x 1 = _____

Add up your totals in the last column = _____

5–8 points: We Should All Have a Friend Like You. You're a true friend. You always have your friends' best interests at heart and go out of your way if any of them ever need you for anything. You value your relationships and will make some lucky guy very happy if you treat him as well as you treat your buddies.

9–12 points: Friend in Progress. You know you're not the greatest friend all the time, but you do strive to be better. And that's what makes you a pretty good friend. Yes, sometimes you can be selfish and self-centered, but you're aware of these tendencies and often try to curb them. Read the tips in this chapter, keep working on your friendship style, and you'll see that all your relationships, platonic and otherwise, will improve.

13-15 points: Friend in Need (of Learning What It Means to Be a Friend). There's just no way to put this tactfully. You are a bad friend. You may be going around complaining about how evil and backstabbing all your friends are, but you need only look in the mirror to figure out why. It's all starting with you. Read this book *very* carefully, because if you're *that* kind of friend, don't expect to find quality guys waiting in line for a chance at a relationship with you.

That *Girl by Association*

Here is where I share a bit of male psychology with you. If you somehow surround yourself with miserable, jealousy-driven people, no guy worth dating is going to feel comfortable among your group. Worse still, he will take one look at your friends and have serious reservations about whether or not he wants to pursue a relationship with you. After all, if you'd pick these people as friends, suddenly he's not feeling very special that you picked him as a boyfriend.

Now, under normal circumstances, I would never suggest listening to a guy who speaks poorly about your friends. But here is the exception to that rule: If you are dating a great guy, who is just as wonderful to you and your family as he is to everyone in his life, he is going to notice if your friends are taking advantage of you or if your friends are generally harmful people. Not because he's smarter, but because he's got a fresh, outsider's perspective, which may allow him to see clearly where you can't, because too much history and emotion may be involved. If he cares for you and speaks up and tells you how he feels about your friends, I suggest you at least listen to what he has to say. If nothing else, it will force you to take stock of your friendships.

Unfortunately, if he's just getting to know you and has not become invested quite yet, he may decide that birds of a feather flock together and not give you much of a chance.

And could you blame him? While there are some genuinely nice women who have mean friends, the problem with these women is that they are not strong enough to stand up for themselves and they don't have the life experience to choose wisely. No guy is so blind that he won't notice that your friends are less than stellar, and once he does, he'll have no choice but to draw some rather unflattering conclusions about you as well.

TOXIC FRIENDS

With friends like these, who needs enemies? Watch out for these six types of toxic friends. Like attracts like. If these are the people you're attracting, check your friendship karma.

- **Underminer:** She takes little digs at your expense. She's always right there with a sarcastic remark, and she never fails to focus on the negative side of your situation. She can even make your new promotion seem like bad news (e.g., "So wait, you have a new title and more responsibility, but no raise?!"). Insecure Girl, watch out—you're the most likely to wind up with these friends, who only increase your insecurity.

- **Phony:** This one loves you so so *soooo* much. She never stops telling you how great you are. How smart. How charming. How lucky she is to know you. And how you two will be best friends forever. And you'd swear she means every word, except when push comes to shove and you actually need her, she's gone like the wind. Drama Queen Girls often fall prey to these types of friendships.

- **Competitor:** You buy a new handbag, she runs out and buys an even trendier, more expensive one. You tell her you like a guy, she tells you that he tried to hit on her last week. And you just can't shake the funny feeling that she's happiest when things are going badly for you because it makes her feel like she's ahead. Whether they're competing about who has the better job or the better boyfriend, both Working Girls and Agenda Girls can fall into these types of competitive friendships.

- **User:** People can and do use one another for all sorts of reasons, but if you suspect that someone's primary reason for staying friends with you is because they stand to gain from your connections, your money, or whatever else you may have going for you, then ask yourself what are you gaining by hanging out with a user. Due to their very low self-esteem, Desperate Girls may try to buy their friends and wind up surrounded by users. When they stop to look around, a lot of Working Girls may also find that most of their friends are actually just business associates trying to network.

- **Suffocater:** This is the friend who can't seem to live without you. She's the one who will call several times a day just to tell you she's bored, and the one who will get upset and make you feel guilty if you're too busy or too ill to meet her for a drink. Yes Girls, who have a tendency to sometimes let people walk all over them, need to be especially careful of friends like this.

- **Frenemy:** You think she's one of your best friends, until you find out that she spilled your intimate secrets to people you barely know, hooked up with your ex-boyfriend, and has generally gone out of her way to make you look like a fool in public. This kind of "friend" can turn you off of friendship for life. Since bad attitudes are contagious and often engender resentment, Bitter Girls and Drama Queen

> Girls frequently find that some of their closest friends
> are actually frenemies.

It's been my experience that some women simply refuse to face the facts about their social circle. I've dated girls in cliques that were so mean-spirited and unsupportive that after a while that kind of toxic interaction came to seem like business as usual. If you're not careful, it's easy to get sucked into the cattiness. Next thing you know, you're going to bed every night worrying if Jane will tell Jill that you said Jill has terrible style and is in desperate need of a new haircut. You know you shouldn't have said it. You know that you're better than that. You know that you're a nice person. But all you can say in your defense is, "Well, it's not my fault. I wouldn't say those things if Jill wasn't such a _____ _____." You only have to watch one episode of an MTV reality show to understand how common it is for so-called friends to constantly gossip about and criticize each other.

Don't be *that* friend! In the end, the only person you're really hurting with all that bad energy is yourself. Take my word, it's going to be pretty difficult to feel like a worthwhile, deserving person when you can't even count on yourself to be decent to your friends.

Mean Girls Are So High School

"I have to admit, I used to be one of the worst offenders. Back in high school and college, keeping up appearances wasn't just everything, it was the only thing. I picked all my friends based on their popularity and looks. Looking back, I realize that we were all really awful to one another. I was always judging my friends if they gained weight or did something I considered stupid (and I considered a lot of things stupid back then), and I lived

in constant fear that they were judging me too. I swear, there were times I couldn't even bring myself to hang out with certain friends until I had lost five pounds. I really thought they'd all be silently making fun of me and getting a thrill out of my misery. Today, I look back and think, *What the hell was wrong with me? How could I have wasted so much time being an idiot?* I love the friends I have now and I know they love me. We accept one another through fat and thin. Thank God, I grew up and got a clue."
—Tari, 27, Dallas, TX

If You Want Good Friends, Be a Good Friend

If you ever catch yourself trash-talking your friends behind their backs, making snide remarks to their faces, and generally doing more harm than good, I have news for you: You are not being a good friend. And you know it. No matter how much you rationalize your actions, your conscience will let you know what's what.

We've all said or done something to a friend that we wish we hadn't, something that somehow jeopardizes their trust in us. If you're honest with yourself, you know the first consequences of any such anti-friend action are anxiety, worry, fear, and general insecurity about the future of your relationship. After all, whether you're talking about romantic relationships or platonic ones, trust is paramount. If you don't trust somebody, is she really a friend? If your "friends" can't trust you, are *you* really a friend?

Once you stop playing the mean-girl game with your friends and the world around you, you'll start feeling good about yourself and become the kind of real person that draws people in with your goodness.

Real friendship is not something to be taken lightly. Next time you are about to say something negative about a friend or make some boastful comment to establish your superiority in the relationship, just don't do it. Count to five and hold your tongue.

I'm certainly not telling you never to poke fun at your friends. Sarcasm and being able to kid around with your friends is essential to keeping friendships upbeat and lighthearted. Just be careful—there is a fine line between sarcastic funny and sarcastic hurtful. If you're not sure where it lies, then stick to making fun of yourself—it's safer!

Great friendships, much like great relationships, aren't born, they're made. Be willing to invest the time and energy to establish true friendships, and in doing so, I guarantee that you will find it much easier to develop an even stronger bond when it comes to the man in your life. Any man that you want to spend your life with will respect that you have great friends. If he is threatened by your friends and creates a me vs. them environment, then run for the hills!

I knew I had a true friend when . . .

"Sometimes, it's the smallest things that make a big difference. I always thought my friend was wonderful, but I didn't realize exactly how great she was until we were sharing a chocolate croissant. I know this sounds silly, but you know how some parts of the croissant have a lot of chocolate in them, and other parts are all croissant and no chocolate? Well, anyway, I would have taken the chocolaty part for myself, but she didn't. She saved the best part for me. I realized then what a good person she is and how much better I could be as a friend. When she had a miscarriage last month, I tried to be the kind of friend I knew she would have been if roles had been reversed. I think I succeeded and our friendship is stronger than ever. I can't tell you how nice it is to have a friend that I can completely depend on and vice versa." —Lainie, 29, San Francisco, CA

Do Good

If you weren't around and someone asked your friend about what you are like, what would you want your friend to say? My guess is that you'd only want her to think the very best of you as a person. Now, how do you go about establishing such goodwill?

Simple. By doing good deeds and being humble about it. I know it sounds old-fashioned. I know you heard it all before in Sunday school. I know it doesn't seem very hip or edgy. Nonetheless, it works. You can't expect your friends to love you just because you share a passion for the same five hot spots. You'll have to do better than that if you want to earn their high esteem.

You cannot put a price tag on how good you feel when you do something generous and kind for friends without expecting anything in return. Don't worry if they're not reciprocating. It could be that they're still operating under the old order. Give them time to adjust. Here are some quick ways to make your friends feel good about you and, in the process, improve your own feelings toward them and toward yourself:

1. If you have something nice to say, say it. From "I love that necklace" to "I love your sense of humor," if you're thinking something nice, go ahead and say it. But only say it if you mean it. I'm endlessly annoyed by women who tell each and every one of their friends how great they look, without ever looking at them!

2. If you don't have anything nice to say, talk about the last episode of *Desperate Housewives*.

3. Next time you go to lunch or take a cab, insist on picking up the tab.

4. If you see a book, a DVD, or something small a friend may

like, get it for them—for no reason other than to say, "I appreciate your friendship."

5. Pick up the phone and call or send an instant message just to see how they're doing. Make sure you ask about their life and don't go on and on about yourself. Friendship is a two-way street, so if you want your friends to be there for you, be there for them.

These are just five small gestures to show your friends that you care—and there are a million more. Here's the bottom line: Until you prove to your friends that they can trust you to have nothing but their best interests in mind, the friendships will be superficial. But once trust is established, that's when you know you've got a true friend. And when you have true friends, men notice.

Who's Your Best Friend?

One of my favorite quotes of all time comes from Abraham Lincoln. It says, ". . . if at the end . . . I have lost every other friend on earth, I shall at least have one friend left, and that friend shall be down inside of me."

This chapter wouldn't be complete if I didn't talk about the importance of being your own best friend. The truth is, you can't always control what other people do. No matter how well you treat your friends, you may still be disappointed over and over again. You are the only person you can control. As your own best friend, remind yourself not to make fun of other people, to always be trustworthy, and to always do your best by your friends. Remind yourself how awful it feels to know that you've done something that may be damaging to your friendship and resolve to do all in your power to never feel that way again.

In the end, it's like Abe said: If you have managed to keep your own trust and respect, you have the friendship of the most important friend you'll ever need. Believe me, the benefits of trusting and respecting yourself will be worth it. Not only will you discover a whole new level of personal satisfaction, but, mark my words, men will suddenly start taking you seriously and looking at you as a person of character and substance. Now, that's the type of woman who is relationship material—not the airhead who would sell her best friend down the river for a shot at the boyfriend!

In the end, by learning how to be a great friend, you are learning how to be a great girlfriend. Ask an elderly couple why they're still happy together and you'll hear the same thing: We are best friends.

Insecure Girl

hanks to my female friends, I learn more and more about women every day. Sometimes, what I find out really shocks me. For instance, I'll never forget a conversation I had with a really attractive friend of mine during which she revealed that when she looks in the mirror, she is constantly disappointed by what she sees. I was confused because I've been out on the town with this girl and she is constantly getting hit on, whistled at, complimented, the works. I thought for certain she knew how good-looking she was. So I reminded her of all the things other people say about her and all the attention she gets.

"Oh, that's just the way guys are," she replied. "They hit on anything that moves."

Well, okay, then . . . what about all the compliments she gets from women?

"They're just being nice."

I couldn't believe it. She had an answer for everything. Yet she couldn't see the one obvious fact staring her in the face that was the answer to my questions—simply put, she is beautiful.

Of course, insecurity doesn't have to be about looks. Many an Insecure Girl thinks she's not smart enough or interesting enough or successful enough to deserve admiration. Unlike the Bitter Girl, who affects an attitude of superiority so she can look down on everyone, Insecure Girl reserves her hostility for herself and puts the rest of the world on a pedestal, often believing that other people know better than her or are somehow more worthwhile.

I've known many Insecure Girls who turn to alcohol and drugs to boost their confidence and combat their social anxiety. I've been on more than a few dates with women who threw back numerous shots of alcohol beforehand. (I presume because some of them weren't sure whether or not their regular personalities would be engaging enough.)

While I completely understand having a glass of wine to relax before a date, the Insecure Girl doesn't seem to grasp that it's perfectly normal to feel nervous anticipation when going out with someone for the first time. As a result, her confidence plummets as her anxiety builds, her nerves overwhelm her, and all her insecurities come flooding out.

That's the sad reality about insecurity—it's a self-fulfilling prophecy. Insecurity gets you focusing on the negatives, which only makes you more unsure of yourself. Worst of all, these worries are usually completely groundless. You're afraid you're somehow not enough, that something is missing—be it a sense of humor, a high IQ, or a stunning bikini body—so you put up a brave front to trick the world and keep others from discovering your true self. The problem is, it's easy to see through the act. Deep down, if you're uncomfortable in your own skin, you're never going to be happy, no matter how many people you think you've fooled.

And as for a solid relationship, you can forget it. If you're Insecure Girl, you have trouble just being yourself because you don't think your real self is good enough. Instead, you try to put on a show and impress us with whatever character you think is most interesting. Can you see why it would take a miracle to make a real connection under those circumstances?

Could You Be an Insecure Girl?

Everyone is a little insecure, but Insecure Girls take the whole self-doubt thing to new extremes. Answer the following questions and find out where you stand on the insecurity continuum.

1. Your best friend has been raving about a new girl she's befriended. Your reaction is:

    a. I wonder if she likes her more than she likes me?

    b. I want to meet this girl and see for myself. How amazing can she be?

    c. I can't wait to meet this great girl!

2. You go out with a friend and she gets a lot of male attention. Your reaction is:

    a. Upset. This is proof that she's more attractive. That's the last time you hit the town with her.

    b. Pissed. She's such a show-off. Of course she's getting attention—she's begging for it with that plunging neckline. Next time, you'll wear your skintight dress and see how she likes it.

    c. Happy for her, but thinking about updating your going-out wardrobe.

3. Your boyfriend is spending a lot of time talking to your best friend. Your first thought is:

    a. If he has so much in common with her, why doesn't he just date her!

b. I wonder if she's flirting with him.

c. How cool—my two closest friends are getting along.

4. You want to try online dating, but before you can, you need to write a paragraph about yourself. You:

a. Decide to forget the whole thing. You have no idea what to say!

b. See what other people have to say, then spend hours trying to write something similar so that you don't sound completely idiotic.

c. Come up with something ridiculously smart, thoughtful, and witty on the spur of the moment, what else?

5. You are most insecure about . . .

a. My relationships. I am not sure if the people in my life really love or like me.

b. Where do I start? The hair on my arms . . . the size of my fat fingers . . . the fact that I have been at the same lame job for five years . . . take your pick!

c. Certain character flaws that I'm working to fix. Those, and the first day back on the beach in a bathing suit.

6. Your date tells you that you look beautiful. You think:

a. Man, this guy must really want to get laid.

b. What a nice thing to say.

c. Score two points for the man with great taste.

7. At work meetings, you:

a. Stay quiet. As the saying goes, "It is better to stay silent and be thought a fool than to speak up and erase all doubt."

b. Sometimes ask questions or make points, but mostly stay in the background.

c. Often take the lead, giving your opinion and trying to get your points across.

8. One of your friends calls you and asks if you're going to a mutual friend's party that night. You haven't heard anything about it. You figure:

    a. She must be snubbing you, and you cross her off your Christmas-card list.

    b. She must have forgotten to invite you, so she can't possibly like you all that much.

    c. It must have slipped her mind, so you call her up to find out what time you should be there.

9. When I go out, I drink:

    a. Like a fish. My personality only shines when I'm drinking.

    b. Until I can finally relax. Then I try to pace myself.

    c. Responsibly. Of course, every now and then I may have one too many.

10. Take one minute to write down everything you love about yourself, from personality traits to physical characteristics. Once your minute is up, count the number of items on the paper:

    a. Zero to three.

    b. Four to six.

    c. Seven or more.

Scoring:

Number you answered with *a*: _____ x 3 = _____

Number you answered with *b*: _____ x 2 = _____

Number you answered with *c*: _____ x 1 = _____

Add up your totals in the last column = _____

10-16 points: Given this score, I'm fairly certain you don't need me to tell you that you're confident. You're one cool, calm, collected woman. Very impressive. Unless of course you were too insecure to answer these questions honestly.

17-23 points: If you didn't already know, you are somewhat insecure. While your condition isn't aggravated, you will want to get to the root of your insecurities and figure out a way to accept and like yourself in spite of your flaws.

24-30 points: It's official. You are the picture of Insecure Girl. Your insecurity is so profound that you doubt everything about yourself, from how you look, to how you speak, to how you look while you're speaking! The rest of this chapter will shed light on why nipping this insecurity in the bud is so vital if you ever hope to establish a meaningful relationship with someone other than Fluffy or Whiskers.

Two Reasons Why Guys Don't Like Insecure Girls

Even in high school, when 99 percent of us were insecure, it was still the more confident girls who always seemed to wind up with the strongest relationships. While there are a million different reasons for this, let's start with:

Reason #1: Confidence is a turn-on. Self-doubt? Not so much.

It never fails. What you think of yourself is ultimately what everyone will wind up thinking about you as well. If you believe you're the coolest thing since the Sub-Zero, your dates are going to feel chills running up their spines in your presence. If you feel that your personality is about as exciting as a slice of day-old bread, you probably won't inspire much passionate devotion on the part of your suitors.

One of life's little realities is that when you question yourself, you leave others no choice but to entertain the same doubts. So instead of feeling attracted to you, he winds up wondering,

Why don't I feel anything? What's missing? And suddenly, it doesn't matter how physically stunning you are. If you're not into you, neither is he. It's that simple.

Reason #2: A conversation with you is like a walk in a minefield.
There are two kinds of people in this world: the simple and the complicated. You definitely belong in the latter category. While simple people are commonly described as "open books" and "what you see is what you get," complicated people are not as easy to figure out. They are often reserved, sensitive, and prone to sudden mood shifts that are inexplicable to the people around them. More often than not, these complications stem from profound insecurity.

One time, I was talking to a girlfriend who was complaining about her weight. I know, I know. I should have just listened and kept my mouth shut. But after going on and on about how fat she was, she mentioned a celebrity, let's call her the "post-Jenny" Kirstie Alley, and said that Kirstie looked great.

"Well," I replied, "if you think she looks great, then why are you complaining about being fat? You're a lot thinner than her."

"Oh, thanks a lot!" she said, really upset. "Now you're comparing me to Kirstie Alley!"

Wait a second . . . did I miss something? Didn't she just say she thinks Kirstie looks great? I never heard the end of it after that. In fact, to this very day, she still reminds me of that comment.

This is just one example of the myriad ways that anything a guy says can and will be held against him in the mind of an Insecure Girl. If he touches on any of her many sore spots, he can just forget about having a good time because he's guaranteed to spend the next two hours in the exhausting and ridiculous exercise of assuring her that he didn't mean it "like that" and that he thinks she's wonderful just the way she is.

I USED TO BE THAT GUY: MY STORY

When I was in medical school, I remember being in awe of my mentors who were so much better and more talented than I thought I could ever possibly be. I believed I'd never be good enough. I actually thought about quitting because I was so sure I'd never measure up. Believe me, there were some dark days filled with self-doubt, and many days and nights in the hospital during which I felt lost, alone, overwhelmed, and insecure. And did I mention afraid?

Today, I know I'm a good doctor. I may not have the encyclopedic memory of Dr. Smith or the perfect technical finesse of Dr. Jones, but I do know my strengths. I do know that over time I have developed a wealth of medical knowledge and, maybe more important, a warm and approachable bedside manner.

I wasn't always this comfortable with myself, but going through all the trials and tribulations of life, med school, a stressful ER, *The Bachelor*, and so on, I've discovered that there is no end to the things you can be insecure about. Some self-doubt is only natural; someone is always going to be better at something than you are. Then, one day, you realize that you don't have to be the best at everything. Life is not a competition. You just have to be comfortable with the effort you're putting forth and what you bring to the table. After that, it all gets easier.

The Dead Giveaways

At heart, insecurity is really just a belief that you're not good enough, for whatever reason. Although you may think people can't tell that you are unsure of yourself, you are communicating with dozens of subtle signals that combine to make your painful insecurity quite clear. Here are just a couple of the dead giveaways:

Dead Giveaway #1: Shy Girl

"People don't always realize it, but I'm very shy. Sometimes, they think I'm snobby or stuck up, but the truth is that it takes a lot for me to open up and trust new people. I don't know why I feel so uncomfortable and clam up in most situations. I didn't choose to be this way, that's just how I am."
—Presley, 21, New Orleans, LA

Since being shy is more socially acceptable than being insecure, I've met many Insecure Girls who prefer to think of and refer to themselves as shy. Sure, some people may jump to the conclusion that you're simply demure, but the smart ones will figure out what your problem is in no time—you lack confidence.

In a way, all of us are surrounded by an invisible force field. If you're shy due to insecurity, that force field repels people. If you're confident, it attracts them. That's why two identical twins can walk into the same room and one will find herself being approached and chatted up by any number of people, while the other will wind up hanging out at the buffet all night.

Dead Giveaway #2: The Eyes Have It

"The sexiest thing about a woman is her eyes. Just one look can say a thousand words. If I'm out with a woman and she's not making eye contact, it's usually very hard to maintain a conversation." —Michael, 26, New York, NY

Anyone who can remember back to their adolescence can probably recall a time when prolonged or direct eye contact made them feel somewhat uncomfortable. Most of us grow out of that phase. Once we are sure of who we are and what we have to offer the world, we feel like we can look anyone square in the eye. Since Insecure Girl has yet to come into her own, she tends to have a lot of trouble in this department.

Darting or downcast eyes, the inability to hold a gaze for longer than a millisecond—these are some of the telltale signs of Insecure Girl. Believe me, when a guy notices that a woman can't look him in the eye, he immediately understands that she is intimidated. It's like two boxers getting into the ring together. They're trying to stare each other down to show that they're tough. If one of them can't even make eye contact, well, he may as well throw in the towel right then and there because that fight is over before it's even begun.

What You Should Be Worried About (and It's Not Your Hair, Hips, or Sense of Humor)

As an Insecure Girl, you have no idea how many of your friends want to shake some sense into you because they see what you can't—that the only thing you're missing is some confidence. One friend of mine routinely complains about her skin, her body, and her career. She's downright compulsive about it. In truth, not only is she attractive, but she's got a warm, completely disarming personality and she's fantastic at her job. If I didn't know better, I'd think she puts herself down to fish for compliments.

Except I do know better. I know that the reason she never goes to the beach is because she doesn't think she looks good in a swimsuit, and that the reason she changes the subject when people ask her what she does for a living is because she really isn't proud of her work as a corporate lawyer. That's what is so tragic about being insecure—missing out on all the fun you could be having because you're too worried about the terrible things other people must be thinking about you.

Unfortunately, missing out on a full life isn't even the worst thing that can happen. When social insecurity leads to drinking and hard partying, the consequences only go from bad to worse. I know many women who will go out on a date and get so drunk that they wind up saying a lot of regrettable things and ruining their relationships. Worse still are the cases I see coming through the Emergency Room: Women who accidentally overdosed on alcohol and other drugs, and victims of sexual assault who were so wasted they don't even remember what happened . . . the stories are frightening and only too common.

DR. STORK'S SOAPBOX: NO WONDER YOU FEEL INSECURE

When it comes to insecurity, we don't have to shoulder all the blame for our inferiority complexes. We're all victims of our society to some extent.

And it's not just women either. As an example, everybody knows that as guys reach puberty, they become extremely concerned about the size of their you-know-what. There are dozens of bogus supplements on the market claiming to make it bigger. You name it, and a marketer somewhere is playing into a man's insecurities about the size of his penis.

I had a friend in high school who got so fed up with this locker room preoccupation that he gave himself the nickname "Half-Inch." And it stuck! Yet, he went on to date and marry one of the coolest, prettiest girls in our school. By laughing at something that has caused so many men so much anxiety, he robbed his insecurities of their power and was able to smile all the way to the altar.

As bad as it is for men, however, our society's tendency to play into women's insecurities is much worse. As a case in point, I've been out with a few women who openly apologize for the size of their breasts. And who can blame them? Every billboard in America seems to show a "perfect" female and women begin to feel they are somehow poorly endowed if they aren't sporting the *Playboy* cover model look. Now, if you think the advertiser's goal is to make you feel anything other than insecure about yourself, think again. I can see it now: "Do You Want to Look Like This? Breast Enhancements, Face-Lifts, Tummy Tucks—Making You Happy Is Our Number One Priority."

Really? If "truth in advertising" was anything more than a contradiction of terms, what that billboard would say is: "Our ultimate goal is to make you feel so bad about yourself that you feel compelled to spend all of your money to feel better."

The sad truth is that without people's insecurities, our entire economy would go up in smoke. Once you're aware of this, you can choose not to buy into it. Remember, nobody is perfect. If there are things in life you aren't great at, so what? Who cares? Life would be boring if everybody was perfect in every category. Instead of dwelling on your flaws, embrace your positive qualities and then surround yourself with people who do the same.

Don't Date That Guy

Conventional wisdom has it that "like attracts like." You can be at a party filled with unconfident people, but if you have high self-esteem you will somehow find the one other person in the place who also has high self-esteem. If you're insecure, however, you can walk into a crowd of self-assured people and you'll still manage to draw one of the following types:

- **Mr. Party Guy:** If you're out drinking to get drunk every weekend and constantly searching for the next high so you can escape your insecurities, you're going to meet a lot of guys who are only interested in partying. For the most part, these aren't sincere or stable characters. And even if your party guy is relationship-minded, he's hardly going to be an influence for clean, healthy living. In fact, once you get your act together, you're going to have your hands full keeping this type of boyfriend sober.

- **Mr. Fix-It Guy:** Sometimes, Insecure Girl has the effect of making people around her feel better about themselves. Guys who date Insecure Girl are usually deriving some satisfaction from feeling like they're helping you realize that you are worthy of a few spare oxygen particles. The problem is they never believe you are their equal and always feel like you need them way more than they need you. Once you get a new attitude and find your inner poise, the dynamics will change and the relationship is destined to crumble.

- **Mr. Insecure Guy:** Ms. Insecure Girl, meet your perfect match: Mr. Insecure Guy. It seems as though insecure women are constantly on the search for a man who will validate them and make them feel better about themselves. Insecure Guy is your knight in shining armor because he'll say anything to pump up your fragile ego as long as you do the same in return. Such relationships often last, but instead of bliss, this couple is shrouded in quiet complacency, never forced to discover the power of inner confidence. Moral of the story: Don't look to Mr. Insecure Guy to save you.

Look On the Bright Side

As someone who is used to looking at the glass as half empty and dissecting everything that's wrong with you and your life, this chapter probably came as no great change of pace. So you're insecure. What else is new? What you may not know is that being insecure has its redeeming characteristics. For instance:

- **You're humble:** Never underestimate the value of humility and modesty. These are the qualities that make it easier for others to relate to you. Nobody likes people who go around thinking they're God's gift to the world. At least you're not out there disturbing the peace with the loud blowing of your own horn like the Drama Queen.
- **You're better than you know:** So many people have exaggerated ideas about their own importance, talents, and skills. But not you. If anything, you're a thousand times better than you give yourself credit for. Once you realize that, imagine how happy you'll be.
- **You're normal:** *Everyone* is insecure to some degree at different points in their life. In fact, some level of insecurity can be a good thing. If you have an important

task that you need to complete, your insecurity about failing to do a good job will provide the adrenaline that you need to give an inspired effort. My first year as a doctor was so tough that every day I'd walk into the hospital hoping I wouldn't screw up. I was insecure in my knowledge. Insecure in my skills. The only way I got through that year with my sanity intact was by talking with my peers, who, you guessed it, had the exact same insecurities. My point is: Ms. Insecure Girl, you're not alone!

Your Rx: Get Comfortable.

If your main problem is a sense of discomfort with yourself, your first step is to admit what's bothering you. Like I said, in this day and age, insecurity is par for the course. But you can overcome it. Over time, the following changes will combine to make you a more confident person:

- **Make a change:** If there are parts of your life that make you uncomfortable, figure out whether or not you can make a positive change. If it's something that you *can't* change, like your height or your impossibly strained relationship with your mother, then your challenge will be to accept the situation such as it is and try to make the most of it. But if you can change whatever is bothering you, then for God's sake, do it! Without some insecurity, no one would ever accomplish anything. So if you're not happy with your professional standing, start putting in more hours at work or looking for a new job. If you're dissatisfied with your look, give yourself a makeover. Change your lifestyle. Then see how much more confident you feel after you've battled your insecurity and won.

- **Buy a new handbag:** Okay, so I'm kidding. I had to make sure you were still paying attention! While there's nothing wrong with making a purchase to treat yourself, a handbag purchase won't buy you inner confidence. Unfortunately, too many people think buying a fancy new car, a bigger house, or, in this case, a handbag, will bring happiness and confidence. Alas, contrary to what our society would like us all to believe, confidence is not on store shelves. But on the bright side, it is free! If you want to feel good about yourself, try volunteering instead.

- **Take good care of yourself:** No amount of money, St. John's Wort, or designer clothes will give you the kind of energy, self-satisfaction, and body confidence that come with a healthy lifestyle. This isn't about weight loss, it's about feeling better, having more energy, and getting out and living. Believe it or not, sometimes half of what I see in the Emergency Room is the effect of depression and other mental health problems. Now I don't know about you, but that's all the proof *I* need that a sound mind and a sound body are a package deal.

As an Insecure Girl, it's possible that you often fall back on alcohol, cigarettes, and other substances to get you through a date or a night of socializing. Unfortunately, this strategy backfires more often than not. I can't tell you how many times I've seen grown women acting like they were at a frat party despite being thirty-five years of age. Not too sexy. If you're

having a hard time maintaining your healthy habits
in social situations, try to . . .
- **Shift the focus away from yourself:** The best way
to quit being self-conscious isn't through a bottle of
wine, but through concentrating on something, or
someone, else. If you are sick to death of worrying
about the impression you're making, just focus on
figuring out what you think of the people you've been
trying to impress. Pretty soon, you'll be too caught
up in conversation to pay much attention to your
self-conscious thoughts.

So next time you go on a first date, instead of spending
three hours focusing on your hair beforehand, spend that
time getting excited about how much fun you are going to
have. Focus on conversation topics that you would like to
engage him in so you're not constantly wondering about
what he thinks of you. When you are at dinner, ask him
questions about his life. Be invested. Be interested. Be positive. And smile. Forget about trying to suck in your stom-
ach, stop worrying about your lipstick, and remember your
attitude is how you present yourself to the world. A smile, a
truly genuine smile, is magnetic and completely disarming.
If you are ever in an awkward dating moment or feel your
confidence waning, just smile. If the guy doesn't smile back,
then he's not worth a second date anyway.

Fake It Till You Make It

I'm not going to sugarcoat this for you—faking confidence is
tough. But it can be done. To be completely honest, you'll have to
work very hard to appear self-assured if that's not how you really

feel deep down. But if you smile a lot and make a habit of doing the following things, you'll be on your way:

- **Count your blessings:** Sitting around and dwelling on the negative is enough to depress even the happiest of people. On the flip side, thinking long and hard about all the great things you've got going for you will have the opposite effect. So start every day by thinking of one personality trait, physical characteristic, or past accomplishment that you can be proud of. While you're at it, always remember to take every compliment you get as the honest truth. Say "thank you" and smile.

- **Psych yourself up:** Before you go into any intimidating situation, be it a date, a party, or a corporate meeting, take some time to give yourself a pep talk. Remind yourself of all the great qualities you possess and then walk into the room pumped with your own hype.

- **Stay sober:** The only way to prove that you can have fun without substances is to try it a couple of times and see what happens. Think about it this way: If you need to get drunk to believe you're having a good time, maybe you're not really enjoying yourself after all, in which case, wouldn't it be smarter just to go home?

- **Confess your secret fear:** If you're the type of Insecure Girl who puts on a brave face but keeps all her fears and frustrations bottled up, it's time to talk about how you really feel. Whether you write down your insecurities in a journal or discuss them with someone you trust, you'll feel a lot better after you subject them to the light of reason by writing them down or saying them out loud.

- **Learn to laugh at yourself:** Like my friend "Half-Inch" proved, the quickest way to lose an insecurity is to gain a sense of humor about it. Whatever your insecurity, whether it's about your looks, your relationship history, or your dance moves, if you're unsure about it, you're in good company. Get together with some girlfriends and laugh about your worries over wine or coffee. As you put your anxieties into perspective, don't be surprised if you soon find yourself feeling a lot less insecure and a lot more confident.

Desperate Girl

Of all *those* girls who you don't want to be or even remotely resemble, Desperate Girl is near the top of the list. Who hasn't heard horror stories and cautionary tales of the dreaded "desperate single woman"? She's the one who's always going around saying, "I need a boyfriend!" Sure enough, in her mind, she believes she needs a man to complete her just as much as she needs food and water to survive. Not only is she not content without a relationship, but somewhere along the way Desperate Girl has decided that her entire existence is nothing more than a waiting period—*real* life won't actually begin until she meets the proverbial "man of her dreams."

Not surprisingly, the Desperate Girl will do anything to get a man. She'll throw on her skimpiest outfits night after night and scour the bars and clubs for Mr. Right. She'll chase any half-decent guy who so much as looks in her general direction. She'll alert everyone she knows, from her real-estate broker to the corner store clerk, that she's single and available for blind dates and setups. She'll write her phone number on walls in the men's bathroom. (Okay, I'm kidding about that last one, but you get the picture.)

Then again, being desperate isn't always a permanent condition. You can be going along just fine on your own, feeling confident and on top of the world, not desperate or even worried about meeting anyone at all. Then, suddenly, *bam!*, you run into some guy who steals your attention as your heart skips a beat. Next thing you know, you're consumed with anxiety at the thought of never seeing him again, and yes, you too become Desperate Girl in an instant. It's what I call "situational desperation," and we've all suffered from its grip. Fortunately, it is usually not permanent—but if you are currently suffering under its throes, this chapter should help get you back to your senses.

Ask most people if they're desperate, and you'll likely hear a big, fat "no." Nobody likes to think of themselves as desperate, but if you've ever picked up the phone, dialed his number, and left a message (or hung up) only to pick up the phone and dial his number again, and again, and again . . . well, then you've known desperate. If you've ever sat at a bar or club waiting for someone, anyone, to come talk to you, wondering, *What the hell is wrong with me that nobody is checking me out*, then you too have been up close and personal with desperation. If you find yourself so afraid of losing a guy's attention that you agree to have sex with him even if you are not ready, then, guess what, you've stolen a page out of the Desperate Girl's handbook.

Now, if your reaction to any of the above was, *Yeah, I've been the Desperate Girl . . . I can't believe I ever acted that way!*, then your desperate days are probably long behind you. If, on the other hand, none of the above sounds remotely familiar, then you're either one of the most self-assured women ever to come into this world or you're in a state of old-fashioned denial. Figure out which is the case by taking the following quiz.

Could you be a Desperate Girl?

Desperate Girls are notorious for lying to themselves. The state of desperation is just so all-around unappealing that many Desperate Girls would rather live in perpetual denial than face the truth. The catch is, if you refuse to admit the facts and continue to rationalize your behavior, not only will you keep acting desperate, but you'll just get worse and worse with each passing year. On that note, please try to be honest when you answer these questions:

1. **T / F**   Sometimes, I feel pressured to have sex and I give in.

2. **T / F**   If I like a man enough, there is very little I won't do for him.

3. **T / F**   Whenever I get involved with someone I really like, I feel like it absolutely has to work out because he might be the only man for me.

4. **T / F**   If it's true that you meet someone when you're not looking, then I'll never meet anyone. I'm *always* looking.

5. **T / F**   I can't imagine being happy without a relationship.

6. **T / F**   After a good date, my cell phone is glued to my hand in anticipation of his call.

7. **T / F**   A woman needs a man. It's that simple.

8. **T / F**   I'm humiliated when a guy dumps me. It feels like confirmation that I am not lovable.

9. **T / F**   It seems like the only men interested in me are total losers.

10. **T / F**   I am usually too busy wondering what the guy I'm talking to is thinking about me—and trying to make a good impression—to give much thought to what I think about him.

Scoring:

0-2 True: Phew! I am relieved to report that desperation is not your primary problem. Check out the rest of the chapter for entertainment purposes only, because I'm probably not going to further enlighten you on the matter.

3-5 True: There's no such thing as being a little bit desperate, so consider this score to mean that you are indeed in dire straits and in need of the help offered in this chapter.

6+ True: While you can't be a little bit desperate any more than you can be a little bit pregnant, you sure can be an extreme case. Fortunately, the desperation in your every look, word, and gesture can be a thing of the past if you read this chapter and start taking some advice.

Two Reasons Why Guys Don't Like Desperate Girls

First, I have to tell you there are a lot more than just two reasons that most guys stay far, far away from Desperate Girl. But in the interest of saving time so that you can get the help you need as quickly as possible, I've narrowed the list down to the top two. I hope these explanations can help shed some light on the psychological effects your desperation has on the men who enter your world:

Reason #1: We Love the Chase.

I realize that women have come a long way and that men are not the only ones who enjoy going after and getting what they want. I understand that it's not fair that men should get to have all the fun while women sit around knitting babies' bonnets and hoping for the phone to ring. And I'm only too sympathetic to your desire to make things happen instead of waiting for them to happen to you. I would be the last person to tell you that you're wrong on any of these counts. However, I will be the first to tell you that you can't control the flow of a relationship all on your own. No one can.

Unfortunately, Desperate Girl can't seem to get the whole "two to tango" idea through her head. Sure, you may understand it on an intellectual level, but when it comes to your behavior, you act as if you can force the relationship into existence by just trying a little harder. No matter how many of your calls go unanswered, you won't accept that he's just not that into you because as far as you're concerned, that's not an option. Instead, you prefer to think that he's just acting strange. *Maybe*, you reason, *he doesn't realize that I'm into him. Aha!* So you flirt even more overtly. You make more phone calls. You bring him home-cooked meals. You wear sexier clothes. You tolerate disrespectful behavior. You swallow your anger because it doesn't compare to your irrational, out-of-control need to get him to like you.

But, of course, there's a catch. Let me put this to you plainly: The harder you try, the more you push him away.

All people, male or female, want the chance to pursue. Being desperate leads you to make all the moves, giving the guy no opportunity to chase you back. Instead, all he can do is run away. It's simple relationship dynamics: One person chases, the other retreats. Watch children in a schoolyard and you'll see that concept play out in living color. If you're the one who is tracking him down all the time, he will be the one who is screening his calls and groaning at the sight of your name on his Caller ID.

Does that mean you have to sit at home, hoping he gets a clue and starts chasing you? No way. The trick is *making* him chase you. Sure, playing a bit hard to get and adopting an "I'm the prize, so catch me if you can" attitude may not come as naturally as, say, being perfectly honest and direct about your feelings. Of course it takes a lot less restraint and self-control to pick up the phone and leave one heartfelt, pleading message after another. And obviously it's easier to let him come over for a booty call whenever he sends a late-night text message. Then again, doing the smart thing is rarely easy. So let that mantra be your guide.

Trust me. Once you learn how to be happy on your own, you'll find that not only do you feel worthy of being pursued, but that you're being pursued more often than ever before. Sure, you won't win them all, but when things don't work out, you'll accept that the two of you are simply different and it just wasn't meant to be. No biggie. Next.

Reason #2: We Hate the Pressure.

There's a reason most people want to be wanted and not needed. The pressure of being so important to someone you don't really know all that well or haven't actually been seeing all that long, well, that's just too much for most men (or women, when roles are reversed) to bear. We all want to feel as if we have the time and space to make our own decisions. And we'd like to believe that if we choose against pursuing the relationship, the person we've been seeing won't go jumping headlong off the Golden Gate Bridge. The second you start acting desperate and clingy, however, the object of your desperate affection will start thinking you're likely to do something drastic (cue *Psycho* shower scene music) and he gets terrified.

Now, instead of having an enjoyable time, he's faced much too early with the prospect of responsibility and commitment. He sees that you have become way too emotionally invested. And he's right. As a Desperate Girl, you're not thinking, *Wow, this could be complicated. How will this affect the great life I've got going so far?*

No, you're probably thinking, *Yay, I met the man of my dreams; my dull waiting period is over and real life is about to begin!* Meanwhile, the guy is terrified about how his life is changing. Since it's too soon in the game for him to know whether it's you or the chase that thrilled him, his thoughts sound more like, *Oh my God. What have I done?*

Worse still, he's suddenly feeling sorry for you. You, the poor soul who somehow thinks that he, of all people, is the answer to your prayers. You, the sucker who has known him for all of five weeks and is already counting on him sticking around for five decades. When this kind of pity takes the place of attraction, you can wave that "love of your life" good-bye, because he's peeling out of there so fast, he's leaving skid marks.

THE TWO SIDES OF DESPERATE GIRLS

For some women, being desperate is a regular state of mind. Others find that desperation comes up and suddenly grabs hold of them seemingly from out of nowhere. In the end, however, all end up pushing away the very thing they want most: Love.

1. The Man-Eater: This type of Desperate Girl has a profile—or three—up on every online dating site. She's gone to speed-dating events and is considering hiring a professional matchmaker. She has joined running clubs and signed up for golf lessons. Never mind that she hates running and thinks golf is boring. She is determined, strong-willed, and desperate in her pursuit. Yet, she is still single and can't figure out why she can't seem to land a boyfriend.

2. The Bunny Boiler: Straight out of *Fatal Attraction* or *Vanilla Sky*, this is the woman who seems perfectly normal at first. Like the Glenn Close and Cameron Diaz characters—or, to reference a real case, that notorious diaper-wearing astronaut who drove from Texas to Florida, sans bathroom breaks, to assault her romantic rival—she may come off as poised, professional, polished, and pulled together, hardly the type who would lose her mind for any Tom Cruise, Dick, or Harry. What her calm facade hides is a woman who can't control her behavior in the face of romantic disappointment. She will call, she will stalk, she will show up at his office, she will claim that she's ill or pregnant, she will even drive hundreds of miles in a pair of Depends . . . anything to get the guy she's convinced is "the one" to fall in love with her.

The Dead Giveaways

When you're desperate, men can usually sense it. We can read it in your eyes, hear it in your tone of voice, and see it in your body language. The desperation screams louder than anything else you may say. Sure, if you're an especially good actress you can often hide your neediness pretty well for the first few minutes, hours, or even days of knowing someone. Still, before too long, you end up saying or doing something that makes your desperation known. Hopefully, afterward you kick yourself for sounding so desperate. (e.g. *I can't believe I actually said, "when?" after he told me he'd call me. I am an idiot!*) If, on the other hand, you have no idea how unattractive your desperate actions appear, you're in some serious trouble. How will you ever learn from your mistakes and stop acting so desperate if you don't even realize how other people perceive your actions?

In the interest of helping you help yourself, I'm going to show you two ways that Desperate Girl gives herself away and sends her man running for the nearest exit.

Dead Giveaway #1: I'll Do Anything

"My last two relationships both started out long distance. I met the first guy while living in Miami. He was in town visiting some friends and we immediately hit it off. The only problem was, he was going back to Sweden in a few days. We tried to keep the spark alive over the phone, but he finally said, 'If we don't live in the same city, this isn't going to work.' That was all I needed to hear . . . I moved to Stockholm that same month. Unfortunately, he wasn't ready for a commitment and I eventually moved to Los Angeles for work. Within a month of moving there, I went back to Miami for a trade show and met another great guy. We started flying cross-country to see each other every few weeks. After about two months, I decided that since I still had lots of contacts in Miami, I would move back. I don't know if this will work out, but you have to take risks in life and always follow your heart. I can't help it. As a woman, I enjoy making sacrifices for a man."
—Alana, 26, Miami, FL

I know Alana pretty well, and trust me when I tell you that this second long distance relationship doesn't look like it's going anywhere either. She doesn't realize that the only thing she is likely sacrificing is her relationship. The thing is, neither of these guys actually went so far as to ask her to move for them. That's right . . . she moved to another country for one guy and then cross-country for another, leaving behind jobs and apartments both times, just to spend more time with men who weren't ready to ask her to move. I can only imagine the pressure and anxiety these guys must have been feeling upon hearing that Alana was relocating to their cities without so much as a discussion.

But the fact that she wasn't formally invited didn't seem to matter to Alana. Her thinking is, *Well, you know how men are. They don't know what they want. Sometimes as women we have to show them.*

Granted, that logic may hold true once in a while, but if you stake your career, your hard-earned money, and your entire lifestyle on showing a guy that you're meant for him, then you're one serious desperado. It boggles my mind to think of the extreme measures Desperate Girls will take for a man. The way many of them behave, you can only draw one conclusion: They think getting the guy is more important than anything else in life.

I'll give you one guess as to how that makes the guy in the situation feel: Happy? Excited? Intrigued? Not quite. How about scared to death!

Dead Giveaway #2: The Wrong Attention

"When I go out with my girlfriends, we're not wearing those micro-minis to impress one another. We all want to meet guys. Otherwise, we'd be renting movies, ordering pizza, and giggling in our pj's all night, not braving the sub-zero elements in a tube top! I think clubs are a great place to meet guys. It's fun. You get to dress up, meet new people, and sometimes you go home together. You never know what that could lead to."—Amy, 22, Chicago, IL

Most confident men implicitly understand that the more a woman relies on her sexuality to get attention, the more desperate she probably is. Provocative dress, inappropriate sexual comments, and/or aggressive flirting let us know you're interested all right—sometimes too interested. Suddenly, we get the feeling that what we think of you is more important to you than what you think of yourself. In other words, you value our attention more than your dignity. If I haven't made my point clear, here it is in a nutshell: Any efforts to be outrageously sexy are unattractive in the long run. The key phrase being "in the long run." If you are only interested in a one-night stand, that's great because that's probably all you're going to find. That or a meathead who cares as much about his own pecs as yours.

When you throw yourself at men, you're sending out two very distinct signals. One says you'll do anything to get us to notice you, and the other says that you don't have any qualities worth noticing other than sexuality.

Sure, these tactics will probably get you noticed by a whole posse of guys who want your phone number. But while your inbox will certainly be crammed with obscene text messages, my bet is that you're not going to be taken home to meet very many nice moms.

Don't take any of what I've just said to mean that you should not be proud of your body or that you shouldn't dress in sexy clothes. Just understand that wearing a sexy outfit is very different than flaunting your body every chance you get. If you're looking for more than a one-night stand, leave enough clothes on for us to use our imagination. Let your confidence guide your sexiness, not just your body. If you have a nice body, trust me, we know!

TRY THIS: INSTANTLY SHAKE OFF THE DESPERATION

Next time you go on a date, remind yourself that you are *not* interviewing for the role of Ms. Right. You are absolutely not allowed to go in with the mentality of "pick me, pick me" or "I hope he likes me." Your attitude has to be "I hope I like him." Tell yourself that with your positive energy and fun, lively vibe, it's you, not him, who is doing the choosing. In fact, if he's cool enough, he may even get a second date with you—if he's lucky.

Take it from a guy who filled the title role on a show called *The Bachelor*—you don't have to be on TV to have your pick. If you go on every date with the attitude that you are doing the choosing, then you'll be in the driver's seat as you try to learn whether or not your dates are serious relationship material, short-term flings, or complete dead ends. However, if you go on dates hoping to be picked, you'll have your hands full just trying to be on your best behavior.

Desperate Times and Desperate Measures

Desperate Girls give whole new meaning to the term man trouble. Ever catch those *Dateline* reports of women bamboozled out of their life savings by an unscrupulous man? Or those frightening news stories of abductions, rapes, and murders that happen because women get pressured into ignoring gut instincts telling them not to get into the car or go up to the apartment of a guy they'd only just met? These types of predators prey on a desperate woman's biggest weakness—the uncontrollable need to be loved and liked.

Please don't take this the wrong way. I am not trying to blame the victims. Far from it. All I am saying is that rapists, con artists, and the like are all cowards. They don't usually prey on the strong. Why bother when weaker people make easier marks?

Desperate Girls are especially easy targets because they don't pay much attention to their own feelings of discomfort. The state of desperation is so uncomfortable in and of itself that Desperate Girls get used to feeling a little bit off-kilter. As a result, they may not notice when their internal alarms are being triggered because something very wrong is going on. These are the girls who wind up confused and disoriented in the Emergency Room, saying, "I don't know what happened. I think I may have been raped."

Don't Date That *Guy*

Just as there's a lid for every pot, there's a Desperate Guy for every Desperate Girl. Although Desperate Guy isn't the only type of guy that would consider dating Desperate Girl, he is, unfortunately, the best of the bunch. Here's a sample roundup of the types of guys you're going to attract if you don't change your Desperate Girl ways.

- **Mr. Desperate Guy:** I am sorry to be the one to tell you this, but yes, this is the best you can do right now. Hey, at least you will both be on the same page. You may not be in love, but you will be content in the knowledge that you are not alone. If this is good enough for you, you're probably not going to get much out of this book, or your love life for that matter. If you want more out of life, however, you'll eventually have to learn to stop acting so desperate. Why not start now?

- **Mr. Abusive Guy:** I knew you thought it couldn't get any worse than Mr. Desperate, but here he is . . . Mr. Abusive. This guy is desperate in an entirely different way. He is desperate to have his ego constantly stroked, and since you clearly think he's the best you can do, he'll be only too happy to agree with you. But since he thinks he could do a lot better, he will criticize you, he will cheat on you, and he will treat you like a doormat because he knows he can get away with it. Then, when he finds greener pastures, he'll skip out without so much as a note. Suffice to say, he is not your Mr. Wonderful.

- **Mr. User Guy:** Often the user and the abuser have a

lot in common, but they're not necessarily one and the same. Whereas the abuser will stick around for a while, the user will get on his way as soon as he gets what he came for. That may be sex, it may be money, or it may be a place to stay for a few days. Bottom line is he'll take one look at you and see that you'll do whatever he wants. And believe me, he'll take advantage of the opportunity and exploit you for all you're worth.

It's Not the End of the World

Right about now, the gravity of the situation is probably beginning to dawn on you. If you're just coming to realize that you are Desperate Girl, you're probably feeling none too thrilled with yourself at the moment. But before you jump to the conclusion that there's nothing redeeming about you, take some time to focus on the positive side of your Desperate Girl experience:

- **Unlimited potential:** Think about it this way—you've made it this far struggling under the delusion that you are somehow incomplete on your own. Imagine how much further you'll go once you're free of that misconception. You haven't even begun to grasp how much you have to offer, and once you do, the sky's the limit.
- **Well-intentioned:** Okay, so sue you, you want love. Of all the things some people are out for—power, money, fame—your primary ambition is to be loved. Hardly a crime if you ask me. Looking for love is a noble and universal pursuit.
- **Selfless:** Although your desire to please others now

comes from the overwhelming need to be liked, the fact that you are so considerate of others will serve you well in the future, when you are no longer quite as desperate for their approval. But for the time being, it's okay to be selfish. You deserve happiness. So stop being so selfless until you've shaken off the desperate frame of mind that's got you running in circles, doing anything and everything just to keep other people from leaving you. Once you're through with always trying to please everyone else, you will emerge not only as a considerate and loving person, but as someone who is far stronger and more interesting than you could have ever imagined. A man will stand beside you because he enjoys your companionship, not because you are his stand-in butler.

Your Rx: Let Your Good Qualities Do the Talking

We've established how unattractive it is to throw yourself at guys. So how do you let us know that you're putting yourself out there and you're a total catch? For starters, you have to start believing in yourself and recognizing that you don't need to make yourself so obviously available. Instead, you need to give the impression that you're happy with yourself the way you are. If you give off this impression, intelligent guys aren't so dense that they won't realize you are content with yourself, with or without them. And they'll be drawn to you.

But before you can convince anyone else how lovable and all-around worthwhile you are, you will have to convince yourself. I realize that sounds a bit obvious, but if you aren't able to recognize and appreciate your good qualities, you're in big trouble. If you haven't figured out why you're great yet, then probably no one else has, either. And no number of voice mails or trips to night-clubs in micro-miniskirts will convey the message the way a little confidence and a sense of independence can.

So, how can you shake off that desperation and develop some self-assurance? First, try to focus on all the things you like about yourself, rather than on all the things you don't. Take a good, long, and, most important, kind look at yourself, and search for your best, most interesting qualities. Are you energetic? Are you talkative? Are you responsible? Are you loyal? Are you honest? Are you caring? Are you helpful? Are you patient? I'm sure the list of positive qualities goes on, so take your time figuring them all out.

If you had trouble coming up with qualities you like about yourself, it may be that you don't know or see yourself well enough or are too distracted by the things you perceive as flaws—and how to cover up said flaws—to notice all the good.

Try this: Remember the last time someone decided you were worth getting to know—a new co-worker, a guy you met at the gym, or even a stranger on a plane who struck up a conversation with you. Concentrate on thinking back to that time. What do you think it was about you that made such a good impression? I guarantee it wasn't a desperate cry for attention.

Once you've discovered that you have many wonderful qual-ities to offer, you'll quickly become an old hand at making the most of your strong suits and be well on your way to believing in yourself. But like I keep saying, none of us is perfect, and in order to avoid regressing back to your old ways you'll eventually have to learn to deal with your flaws and not try to mask them with desperate behavior.

You'll be able to accept some of your flaws and live with

them without a problem. Maybe you recognize that you're overly competitive. If you can live with that, you will probably decide that this quality gives the fabric of your personality some interesting texture. Then again, you'll also come across problems that are persistent sore spots. When that happens, give yourself some tough love and a swift kick in the keister.

It may be that you're a smoker and feeling unhealthy, so you insist that you quit. (If you need some motivation, how about this: Each cigarette can take twelve minutes off your life. So you live a shorter life and all the while, due to premature skin aging, you look older. Isn't that reason enough to call 1-800-QUIT-NOW?) It may be that you're a procrastinator and not getting enough done, so you motivate yourself to get up earlier to get more accomplished. Or maybe you notice that your life is humdrum and lacks excitement, so you pick yourself up off the couch, turn off the TV, and start looking into more adventurous ways to spend your free time.

The old you wouldn't be able to face her flaws without losing faith in herself and resorting to obsessive behavior. The new you will know better. Best of all, once you have gained your own love and respect, you won't be so desperate to win the love of others.

Fake It Till You Make It

It's like I've been saying all along—you need to listen to yourself. I realize that's easier said than done when you still haven't found your voice. But following other people can lead you into some serious trouble. Working night shifts at the ER, I've seen what can happen when a woman becomes desperate for a man's attention, and it's not pretty. I don't want you to have to go through anything nearly as disheartening.

Here are a few tricks to help you quit acting desperate in a hurry. While what you're about to read may seem like I'm advocating playing games, which might be frowned upon in some cases, what choice do you have? If you're Desperate Girl, the last thing you want to do is let people know the truth. Instead . . .

- **Get a New Attitude:** Your new motto should be "I can take it or leave it." Just keep repeating it and acting as if you believe it—even if you don't. It may help to invoke the name of your coolest girlfriend— you know, the one who has a line of guys at her beck and call. When in doubt, ask yourself: "What would *[insert name of cool friend here]* do?" These little reminders will make the next four tips a bit easier to pull off.

- **Don't Call Him:** While you're getting your act together and shaking off your desperation, it's best you stay away from pursuing men all together. Once you're on your feet and needy no more, you'll be able to pick up the phone and call to say "hi" without coming off like a man-chasing stalker. Until then, put down that cell phone.

- **Just Say No:** Okay, maybe not *just* no. That would be rude. Try any or all of these polite versions: "Can't. I'm exhausted." "Would love to but made other plans." "Sorry. Tonight's no good. How 'bout a raincheck?" I'm serious. Do it just for practice. Say it, write it, or text it in response to anything from a last-minute dinner invite to a late-night action request. Just say no and leave it at that. If he doesn't follow up, forget it—you haven't missed out on any great opportunities. Trust me!

- **Enforce the Ten-Minute Rule:** Next time you meet a guy you like and start chatting up a storm, take a look at the time. After ten minutes, make an excuse and get out of there. This rule should also be applied to the phone. After ten minutes, plead a previous engagement and disengage. Again, while you're still on the road to becoming un-desperate, always be the first to say good-bye. I know this sounds like playing games, but until you are truly confident and can avoid games altogether, you deserve to be chased for a while!

- **Get Out of the Game:** Sit on the sidelines for a week or four. Just forget about your search for love for a while. Spend time with your family. Bond with your friends. Reconnect with your dog. Catch up on the latest blockbusters. Pick up that book you've been meaning to read. See how much fun you can have without a boyfriend or without constantly searching for one.

Working Girl

U p until now, we've talked about a few different ways to avoid being *that* girl. Maybe you recognized yourself in one or more of these chapters. If not, maybe it's because you're more of a Working Girl. There isn't much love-life feedback you can give to women who fall into this particular category for one simple reason—it's tough to provide feedback on something that barely exists.

The type of Working Girl I am referring to is not the highly functioning career woman who has managed to strike a healthy balance between her professional and her personal life. No, the woman I'm talking about is the one who hides behind her career so she doesn't have to deal with the messy and unpredictable world of dating and relationships. Or, if she's not hiding, she's genuinely so invested in her job that she just doesn't make time for relationships.

As she climbs the corporate ladder year in and year out, she forbids something as silly as a personal life to get in the way of kicking some ass in her career. She's the one who spends most of her waking hours toiling away at work for years on end, only to wonder how it could be that she's still single. But you can tell that she's using her job as an excuse—whether she means to or not—to avoid getting involved with a guy when she says one of her catchphrases:

- "Men are intimidated by my success."
- "I have no time for dating."
- "My work fulfills me completely."

As a doctor, I understand Working Girl all too well. When you're dedicated to your career, a social life is often the first thing to go, and my experience has been no different. I remember one year in particular when I was working at Vanderbilt University in Nashville, Tennessee. I was so consumed by work that I don't think I went on a date for more than a year. I'd go to the hospital, come home, hang out with my dog, and then do it all over again the next day. My family and friends used to joke that I was always either working, sleeping, or hiking with my dog, Nala. With the hours I was keeping, I barely had any time to maintain my pre-existing relationships, much less pursue new ones. I was the quintessential Working Guy. I ignored my dating life.

Luckily, that was when *The Bachelor* came along and changed my entire perspective.

After being approached in a restaurant by a casting agent after a busy day in the ER, I initially laughed at the concept of going to Paris to be *The Bachelor*. My first response: Thanks, but no thanks. As flattering as it sounds, I have a career and there is absolutely no way I'm going to fly off to Paris on a whim. I'm a doctor, for goodness' sake. What will my patients and peers think of me running around in a foreign country with dating women as my sole purpose? I'm Working Guy, I don't ignore the demands of my job for selfish, frivolous fun.

Fortunately, I have wonderful friends, family, and coworkers who were extremely supportive and encouraged me to take the chance. Maybe they knew something I had forgotten: Working in a hospital isn't all I have to offer. And once I took the plunge, so to speak, my life went from all work to all play in the span of a few days. Being in Paris forced me to think about relationships day in and day out. The subject was no longer a lock box that I could hide in the corner while I focused on my medical career. Going to Paris was a life-changing experience. Putting all that time and energy into thinking about what I'm looking for in a partner opened my eyes to what I really want out of life beyond a career. I had been ignoring my love life to the point that I had almost forgotten what I was missing out on. After that experience, I know I'll never downplay the importance of a relationship again. I can say unequivocally that establishing a fulfilling, meaningful relationship with a woman in this life is as important to me as anything else. And even though my career as a doctor has made that task difficult at times, it is absolutely possible. It just takes a fine-tuned balancing act.

Of course, that's just me. You may not feel the same. You may be at a point in your life when you honestly have no interest in relationships and are content to focus on work. But if there's even a slight chance that you're avoiding relationships because work comes easier, then the last thing I want you to do is kid yourself into believing that you're completely satisfied, like I did before *The Bachelor* helped me realize the truth. That would be settling for way less than what you deserve, and I wouldn't be doing my job as the author of this book if I didn't help you figure out how to get what you really want. I don't want you to wake up on the day of your retirement to the realization that your career has not satisfied your inherent need for companionship.

Are You a Working Girl?

This chapter isn't about telling you to cut back on work. I would be the last guy to recommend something like that without knowing you and what you want. That's what this quiz is for. Answer these questions and see for yourself whether you're on track to get what you need out of life:

1. If I never get married or have children, I'll be:
   a. Devastated. I'll feel like I missed out on life.
   b. Fine, I suppose. But I don't know. It's hard to say for sure right now.
   c. Great. Who needs all that extra responsibility and aggravation?
2. Which of the following gives you the most joy?
   a. Being in love
   b. Family and friends
   c. Career
3. If you had a great job offer that required leaving your city and boyfriend behind, what would you do?
   a. I'd decline the offer.
   b. It would depend on where I saw the job and the relationship going.
   c. I'd take the job.
4. You've been looking forward to having dinner with some friends at a hot new restaurant, but a work emergency comes up and forces you to cancel. You:
   a. Try to fix the problem as quickly as possible so I can still meet my friends for drinks afterward.

b. Reluctantly cancel my evening plans and settle in for a long night of work.

c. Feel a jolt of adrenaline as I attack the challenge at hand.

5. If you married and had children, you would ideally:

a. Stay home until they're grown.

b. Work from home, or get part-time hours.

c. Hire a great nanny.

6. Which of the following gives you the most anxiety?

a. Biological clock

b. Public speaking

c. The glass ceiling

7. If you could, you'd work:

a. A few hours per week at most, and that's only so I could appreciate my free time.

b. A standard workweek.

c. All the time. I'm a workaholic.

8. You work mostly for:

a. Income

b. Personal satisfaction

c. Recognition

9. When it comes to your work, which *Sex and the City* character are you most like?

a. Charlotte, the art gallery director who retires when she marries a doctor with "family money."

b. Carrie, the writer who loves the flexibility and creativity of her job.

c. Miranda, the law partner who cuts her hours to fifty-five per week after she has a baby.

10. How long has it been since your last date?

a. A few weeks or less

b. Within the last month or two

c. More than two months

Scoring:

Number you answered with *a*: _____ x 1 = _____

Number you answered with *b*: _____ x 2 = _____

Number you answered with *c*: _____ x 3 = _____

Add up your totals in the last column = _____

10-16 points: You might be working, but you're no Working Girl. If you've been finding that most of your time is being taken up by your job, it's either because you need the money or are paying your dues early on in a career. Your priorities lie in the realm of relationships and you'll do what you have to do to make sure your personal life doesn't suffer.

17-23 points: You love your work, but not to the exclusion of everything else in your life. Still, you are in some danger of letting business get in the way of pleasure and then regretting it down the line. If your personal life hits a rough patch, you're only too likely to use work as a coping mechanism. Take care that this tendency doesn't become a long-term habit.

24-30 points: Going by your answers, you are the prototypical Working Girl. Either you're not at all interested in anything other than getting to the top—in which case, keep it up, you're on the road to great success—or you mistakenly believe that while you have to work at your career, your relationships and personal happiness should either come naturally or not at all. If you think you may fall into the latter category and don't want to end up with a lifetime of regrets, pay extra-careful attention as you read this chapter.

Two Reasons Why Guys Don't Like Working Girls

When it comes to Working Girls, the roles are suddenly reversed and men find themselves in somewhat uncharted territory. While, for the most part, we love driven, successful women, I'm not going to lie—a busy working woman can be intimidating. If you're dealing with a man who lacks confidence, your passion for work may even scare him off altogether. Don't give those guys another thought. I'm more concerned about the secure guys who actually want a chance to date you but have a hard go of it because:

Reason #1: Nobody wants to come second.

Two workaholics who somehow manage to find each other can have a match made in headhunters' heaven, but if you wind up with a guy whose love for his job pales in comparison to yours, be prepared for some difficulties. For instance, Working Girls tend to miss dinner dates, bail early on evenings with friends, pass out at the beginning of every movie, interrupt conversations to conduct important business on their BlackBerrys, and generally engage in any number of behaviors that are usually interpreted as: "I value work more than you."

Like I said, if you wind up with a fellow workhorse, he probably won't notice, much less mind, the implication. However, if you're dating someone who is looking to invest as much energy into his relationship as he does into his work (or more), these kinds of habits are likely to land you back on solo ground before you know it.

Reason #2: How can we meet you if you're chained to your desk?

On the job, Working Girls have their act together. On the interpersonal front, all that savoir faire might go right down the drain.

Suddenly, you go from sitting on top of the world and being able to move mountains, to feeling like a powerless and insecure adolescent. Who can blame you for wanting to stick with what you're good at?

While it's perfectly normal for someone like you to shy away from relationships, don't let your fears sideline you from the dating game. If you never unshackle yourself from your desk, not only is it virtually impossible for us to run into you, but you become so unaccustomed to flirting that if we do have a chance encounter, the experience can end up awkward and strained.

It stands to reason that if you only meet one interesting guy per year because you're so busy at work, you'll likely put way too much pressure on that relationship, thereby driving both yourself and your date up the wall. On the flip side, if you're out and about, meeting all sorts of different men and growing used to the attention, you'll be experienced enough to know what to do when you meet the right one.

The Dead Giveaways

It doesn't take a neurosurgeon to spot a Working Girl. You wear your career like a badge of honor and take pride in your accomplishments. Your work translates into the clothes you wear and the people you surround yourself with. No two ways about it, your job constitutes a substantial part of who you are. While there's nothing wrong with any of this, the extreme cases can be uninviting. Take, for instance:

Dead Giveaway #1: Living to Work

"I love being a publicist. If it wasn't for PR, I don't know where I'd be. My friends, my social calendar, and my every other conversation all center around my clients. I date here and there,

but I haven't had a relationship in years. I need someone who not only understands my hectic schedule, but can also fit into my world, and those kinds of men are hard to find."
—Leslie, 28, New York, NY

When I first met Leslie, she had just moved to New York from Florida and was desperate to make it as a publicist. She once told me, without a trace of irony, "My biggest problem is that in Florida, people work to live. But in New York, everyone lives to work. I'm trying to be more like the New Yorkers."

I told her right then and there what I thought: that living for work isn't the answer and that there's much more to life than our jobs. Years later, she doesn't regret her decision to ignore my advice, but she's definitely a Working Girl. This isn't a matter of right versus wrong. The truth is, she's very happy with her life. However, you cannot have a conversation with her without hearing an exhaustive rundown of her professional triumphs. And you cannot introduce her to new people without hearing her quickly and expertly steer the conversation toward the topic of careers. Any guy can tell right away what matters to Leslie, and I've met more than a few who were turned off by her single-mindedness.

A Working Girl is different than any other type of woman I have ever met in one obvious way. She prefers to talk about work versus relationships. She rarely even mentions guys in conversation unless one is a man she works with. I've known many a Working Girl and have great admiration for them, but I am always questioning why they rarely want to talk about relationships. Quite a role reversal if you ask me! The obvious question for Working Girl is, "Don't you care about finding love?"

Dead Giveaway #2: Always Networking

"Ever since my friend graduated from film school, she's been impossible to hang out with. It's gotten so I can't even invite her to a party. She never shows up anywhere without one of her spec scripts and she's always talking about work and trying to get funding for her movie projects. I don't know. Maybe this is the way it's done. Maybe she's going to become a big success, but she's going to lose all her friends along the way."
—Jessica, 34, Los Angeles, CA

Another obvious sign that you're dealing with a Working Girl is her inability to downshift into social mode. If Jessica's friend sounds a little like you, you may be so wrapped up in work that you confuse socializing with networking.

I often run into women like this, and while I'll agree that drive and ambition are attractive, the Working Girl can go overboard to new extremes. As a doctor, for instance, I wouldn't go to a dinner party with the primary intention of recruiting new patients. Now, if someone asked what I did and wanted my card so they could refer a friend, that would be great. I would be honored to take care of their friend, but I wouldn't exactly try to drum up business at a friendly, informal gathering. Talk about awkward.

My advice? Play it cool. If someone asks, tell them about your career, but unless they show genuine interest, find another topic to talk about.

The Downside of Working Girls

Another way to describe Working Girls is as workaholics. Unfortunately, it's all too easy to rationalize your addiction to work as simply having a good work ethic. But you know the truth: Work becomes a crutch that allows you to avoid issues in your life. Or worse yet, allows you to ignore your personal life altogether.

Your personal life and your love life are likely to be the first to suffer from workaholic ways. Eventually, however, putting work above all else can begin to wear down your health and your state of mind. If you can't turn off thoughts of work once you leave the office, you may wind up fatigued and unable to sleep. If you never learn to delegate tasks because you believe that "if you want it done right, better do it yourself," you stand the risk of acquiring stress-related health conditions like high blood pressure or a myriad of physical complaints that always seem to accompany a stressful, unbalanced life. Abdominal pain, headaches, chest discomfort—I've seen all of these symptoms and more in the ER, and oftentimes the cause is artificial—quite simply, stress. Not to mention the psychological impact of waking up someday, having reached the pinnacle of your profession, only to realize one thing: Your social skills outside of work have grown rusty and, frankly, you're lonely.

Not to be a downer, but let's face it, work can only take you so far. If you're a Working Girl who toils to avoid loneliness, please consider how you'll feel when it's time to retire. Will you look back with regret at not having had a personal life? Or will you be satisfied because you focused solely on work-related success? Only you know how to answer that.

Don't Date That Guy

I get it, you've got a great job. You're independent. You don't need a man to support you financially. I can respect all of that. What I can't respect are some of the guys you might wind up with if you don't stop and figure out exactly what you're looking for in a relationship. Take these two common examples:

- **Mr. Deadbeat Guy:** This is the prototypical slacker who is used to letting others foot the bill for him. He may be an aspiring artist, a perpetual student, or just a chronically unemployed charmer. Whatever he does, the one thing he doesn't do is pay rent. He's the one looking for a Sugar Mama, and a Working Girl is a pretty damn desirable giver of sugar. She has lots of money to support the men in her life and she's never around to nag.

- **Mr. Just Passing Time Guy:** He knows you're into your job, and he wouldn't have it any other way. After all, it's not as if he has any intention of ever actually settling down. This guy is only too happy to play second fiddle to your career, because then he doesn't have to worry about hurting you when he leaves. He enjoys nice dinners, noncommittal sex, and an easy exit strategy.

Employee of the Year

Although I've spent more than a few paragraphs laying into Working Girls, the fact is that I have nothing but admiration for anyone who goes out there and applies themselves on a daily basis. Again, my only intention here is to make sure you're not missing out on a love life, provided that is what you really want. We'll talk more about how to balance down the line, but in the meantime, let's just take a moment to consider a few of the many characteristics that make you pretty amazing just the way you are. You're:

- **Tough:** No matter what your business, it takes strength and discipline to succeed. If you use these qualities to your advantage on the personal front, you'll be a success across the board.

- **Ambitious:** You have big dreams and impressive aspirations. Anyone who is with you will feel elevated and inspired by your dynamic energy.
- **Independent:** You rely on yourself to get things done at work and in life.
- **Dedicated:** If there's anything you understand, it's the value of commitment and hard work. You put everything you have into every project.
- **Competent:** Your confidence is real because it comes from success. You know you're good at what you do, and it shows.

Your Rx: Play Hooky

If your career has been the great love of your life and you're ready for a change, your first order of business should be to start thinking less like an employee, manager, entrepreneur, or boss, and more like an adventurer. Your work ethic is firmly ingrained already. We know you work hard—now learn how to play hard, by:

- **Exploring your passions:** When was the last time you were truly excited by something other than work? My challenge to you is to create a new adventure for yourself that takes you completely away from work. Go somewhere your BlackBerry is not allowed. Plan a Caribbean scuba vacation. Or what about sea kayaking off the coast of Belize? Rock climbing? Badminton? Okay, maybe not badminton, but you get the picture. It's time to start planning your next great adventure. Once you figure out what really gets you going, you'll be able to talk about

something other than just work, and chances are
you'll be more relaxed.

- **Just saying yes:** Not long ago, a friend told me
about a memoir she was reading written by a woman
who decided to spend a year saying yes to every guy
who asked her out. In that time, the protagonist goes
on innumerable adventures, gets in touch with a
wide variety of cultures, and even meets her current
husband—all without even leaving her city. While
I'm not recommending that you follow her lead and
date every Joe Blow who asks, I am suggesting that
you make a concerted effort to say yes to every friend
and acquaintance that invites you anywhere.

Although some of your outings may wind up seeming more
like chores, I'll go five-to-one that you'll also wind up meeting
interesting new people and learning a whole lot more about yourself and the world outside of your job.

Toward the same end, take recommendations seriously—
starting with this one: From now on, whenever someone suggests
you read a book, see a movie, or go to an exhibit, make a note
of it and then go do it! Take two months to live the life of "yes"
and you'll find that you don't have to travel very far, spend a lot
of money, or risk physical injury to make your life exciting. Once
you start saying yes, you'll find plenty of adventure right outside
your office door.

Fake It Till You Make It

If the old "all work and no play" grind is beginning to wear on
you, it's time to switch gears. Of all the personalities we've dis-
cussed so far, Working Girl is by far the easiest to fix. As the

tough, action-oriented woman we just described, you won't have any problems juggling a few of your priorities around to make some quick room for:

- **Online dating:** Perfect for workaholics, the online dating model allows you to read men like résumés and then decide whether or not to hire them for the job of your date. You can also measure and control the amount of time you want to devote to dating each week.

- **Non-work-related conversation:** Next time you're in a social setting, simply refuse to tell anyone who asks what you do for a living until you know each other better. Not only will you seem a lot more mysterious and interesting, but it will force you to make conversation that has absolutely nothing to do with your career. This is a great way to start thinking about where your work ends and you begin.

- **Actual phone calls:** As in, leave the BlackBerry at home. Please, for all our sakes. Your friends are sick of e-mails and texts. They want to hear the sound of your voice, so make some time to talk and *call* them . . . that's right, the way they did in the 1990s.

- **Relax:** Try to relax and enjoy life a little bit! Your job is only as stressful as you make it.

Is your job difficult? Yes. Time consuming? Yes again. Stressful? . . . What if I told you that the answer to that question is partly up to you? Every job has its stressors, but if you can become calmer and less frazzled in matters related to your work, you will have more energy to devote to your personal life. And who knows, maybe you'll become even more effective in your career as you develop a better balance. The next time you find yourself stressed at work, go for a short walk and take some deep breaths. Working in the ER, I've learned that when someone's life hangs in the balance, cool, calm, collected doctors are *much* more effective than frantic, stressed-out balls of nerves. And they are a lot more fun to go have breakfast with after the night shift ends.

Lost Girl

Lost Girls defy definition. They come in all shapes and sizes and personalities. Still, they all sound a lot like this:

- "But I love him."
- "What would I do without him?"
- "I can't seem to let go."
- "If you only knew him like I know him."
- "Why can't it be the way it was in the beginning?"
- "Why would he do that to me?"

Sound familiar? Of course it does. While there are plenty of women who aren't Drama Queens, Desperate, or Bitter, at one point or another, almost every single woman I know has been in a dysfunctional relationship where she *lost* herself. The dictionary defines "lost" as disoriented, off course, adrift, confused, forlorn, aimless, and—the one that really hits the nail on the head—alone. That's what all Lost Girls have in common:

Even though they may be in a relationship, they feel *alone*.

I know I started off the book saying that sometimes it's not him, it's you. And if you're a dead ringer for any of the Girls in the previous chapters, then I stand by my original opinion. However, if you're more of a Lost Girl, it could very well be *him*.

Unlike the Girls in the other chapters, who can often be found sitting around, wondering what's wrong with men and why a wonderful catch like them isn't getting snapped up, you're probably sitting around wondering what's wrong with you and what you did to make your boyfriend act as if you had kicked his dog or mocked his manhood.

I've seen it happen to so many of my female friends. (And, believe me, it happens to men as well!) The relationship starts off well enough, but eventually, things head south. He starts calling her less and canceling plans. Or he becomes emotionally distant and aloof. Sometimes, he turns critical and puts her down. Other times, he may say he has doubts about the relationship—or he may never say anything about doubts, but then one night, out of the blue, he cheats on her. Basically, he does everything to push her away short of actually making the decision to break things off.

However he chooses to pull back, the Lost Girl's reaction is often the same—she blames herself and, as she calls it, begins to "work on" the relationship.

After a while, she's miserable and confused. Her friends barely recognize her. Her family is worried. And her coworkers are tired of hearing the same sob story over and over again. That's what happened to my friend Julie. For more than a year, she felt good about her boyfriend and secure in her relationship. Then she found out that he'd started cheating on her. Did she walk out on him like so many of us suggested? Did she refuse to speak to him until he realized how much he'd hurt her and had done everything in his power to win her back? No. Instead of doing any of that, she decided to "fight for her relationship" by making him home-cooked meals, running his errands, writing him love letters, and doing everything she could to prove her value to him.

Big mistake. That wasn't the first time I've seen a guy similarly rewarded for cheating or misbehaving. And, unfortunately, the only thing this reaction proves to a guy is that he can have his cake and eat it too. After all, men in their purest form are pretty simple creatures. They'll do things that bring them a reward. So, if a guy can have a girlfriend and mess around with other women at the same time, then that is what many men will do. Moral of the story: You can't reward the type of behavior you're trying to prevent.

Are you a Lost Girl?

The path from self-confident to dazed and confused can involve thousands of little steps. These changes can be so subtle that you may not even realize that you've completely lost your center until it's too late. Answer the following questions honestly to figure out if your relationship is what's holding you back:

1. As far as relationships go, yours is:
   a. Pretty wonderful
   b. About normal
   c. Worse than average
2. Your family and friends think your boyfriend is:
   a. Amazing. Just like one of the family.
   b. Okay, but they're happy just as long as you are.
   c. Absolutely wrong for you.
3. If this relationship doesn't work out, you'll:
   a. Be heartbroken, but wiser for the experience.
   b. Be annoyed at having to date again. It's a jungle out there!

    c. Probably never meet anyone again and die alone.

4. When it comes to arguments, I try to:

    a. Hear him out to understand his point of view.

    b. Hear him out so I can use what he says to prove how wrong he is.

    c. Hear him out so I can figure out what he wants and give it to him.

5. You're a half hour late to meet your boyfriend for dinner due to a crisis at work. When you get there, he flies off the handle and tells you that you're completely inconsiderate. You try to calm him down, but he's determined to stay mad. You:

    a. Cancel your evening plans. You'll speak when he's had a chance to cool off.

    b. Get mad right back and spend the night arguing.

    c. Agree that you've been inconsiderate, promise you'll change, and ask him to forgive you.

6. How often does your boyfriend do what you want to do?

    a. All the time. He loves to make me happy.

    b. Once in a while.

    c. Only when he's feeling guilty about something.

7. He makes you feel like:

    a. A princess

    b. An equal

    c. A maid

8. When was the last time you two genuinely had a good time and were completely happy being together?

    a. The last time we were together.

    b. It hasn't been that long. I don't know, maybe a week or two?

    c. It's been so long, I barely remember.

9. Most of the time, I feel:

a. Content and secure

b. Half the time I'm satisfied, half the time, I'm not sure what I want.

c. Stressed and miserable

10. I am with him because:

a. He makes me feel great.

b. He's a good guy.

c. I can't seem to let go.

Scoring:

Number you answered with *a*: _____ x 1 = _____

Number you answered with *b*: _____ x 2 = _____

Number you answered with *c*: _____ x 3 = _____

Add up your totals in the last column = _____

10-16 points: The only person who's lost around here may be your boyfriend. Man, is that guy in love with you! Good for you. Lucky for him, it seems like you're both on the same page. If you two are still in the beginning phase of your relationship, the best advice I can give you is to try to keep your feet on the ground while you enjoy being happy in your relationship. Just don't forget that long-term, stable relationships are a marathon and not a sprint.

17-23 points: There are days when you don't think you know what you want, where you're going, or even if this is the relationship for you. Sometimes, you suspect that he feels the same way. These doubts are a normal part of committed relationships. After all, the fireworks can only last so long. All the same, be careful that you are not sticking around purely out of guilt and obligation.

24-30 points: You're a bona fide Lost Girl. Somehow, you've allowed your sense of right and wrong to slip away, and you no longer know your ups from your downs. You probably started out relatively happy and self-assured, but somewhere along the way, your relationship went from romance to psychodrama. The time has come to stop trying to save your relationship and start trying to save yourself!

Two Reasons to Find Yourself Again

You can stay in your relationship and try to prove your worth to your boyfriend. *Or* you can get out and prove your worth to yourself. If this sounds like a hard decision, we've got our work cut out for us. Here's a truth you may not want to hear: Until you value yourself, nothing you do for him will convince him that you're worthy. So stop pressing his shirts and put away that ironing board, because if you ever want to find your way, you're going to have to do it alone. Here's why:

Reason #1: Men need to be held accountable.

If you consistently let your significant other get away with bad behavior, he will begin to think of you as weak, and you will lose his respect faster than you can say, "What would you like for dinner tonight?" Once this happens, the relationship is just sputtering toward its inevitable demise. You may feel like you're making progress or trying to resuscitate the connection by going out of your way on his behalf, but all you're really doing is beating a dead horse.

When you're going out of your way for a guy, all you're showing him is how worthy he is. If you allow him to get away with doing little to nothing for you in return, your message is loud and clear: He is important, but you are not. You probably already know all this, but if that's the case, why are you still there? If you've already allowed him to walk all over you, the damage is done. Your only option now is to get out and stay out. Take it from a guy, there's no way he's going to come around any other way.

Reason #2: A relationship is only a means to an end.

Why do people get involved in relationships? Is it to have someone around all the time, or is it to feel loved and cared for? When you're in a bad relationship, your emotional needs are not being met. You're always looking for something and never getting it. It's a constant pursuit that never pays off. Eventually, feeling miserable begins to seem normal.

What you want is a companion, someone who makes you feel secure. If what you've got is just some guy taking up prime space on your couch and laying claim to your remote control, then not only do you not have what you want, but you've cut yourself off from the possibility of ever getting it. Even if you two stay together, you'll always feel alone. And that's the kind of loneliness I wouldn't wish on anyone.

The Dead Giveaways

The biggest problem with being a Lost Girl is that while everyone around can see that you're falling for the Wrong Guy, you're too disoriented to know it. After all, the Wrong Guy, just like the Lost Girl, comes in all shapes and sizes. It's sometimes hard to convince yourself that he's wrong for you. Whether it's because he's noncommittal, irresponsible, unfaithful, or abusive, the bottom line is, he is hurting you and undermining your self-esteem, and over time, this type of relentless assault on your sense of self translates into an obvious change in your outlook and personality. You can stop forcing a relationship with the Wrong Guy before it goes any further by looking out for the following dead giveaways:

Dead Giveaway #1: Your friends can't stand him

"My friend was always in control in her relationships, but then

she met Tom and her entire personality changed. He was so sarcastic and rude. He'd criticize her cooking in front of everyone, take an awful tone with her, and ignore her when she asked him questions. If she ever defended herself, he would get mad and it would turn into a fight that would end with him storming out and her in tears. What an asshole! Half the time, I want to reach over and strangle him. I'm invited to their wedding. They want an RSVP, but all I feel like sending are my condolences. I can't imagine what she's in for."
—Kendra, 25, Boca Raton, FL

When the relationship becomes so toxic that outsiders can tell exactly what your personal problems are, it's time to cut and run for your life. If you find your friends putting you in the awkward position of having to defend your boyfriend, the last people you should blame are these concerned friends. Since you can pretty much bet the ranch that this isn't the type of conversation anyone wants to have with you, the only person who you should fault for putting you into this situation is your boyfriend.

Pay careful attention to how often you try to rationalize your boyfriend's behavior. "He's stressed at work." "His mom is crazy, of course he's going to have issues." "I'm sure he *wanted* to get me a birthday present." "He only meant to push me a little." And the next time you hear yourself doing it, for God's sake, snap out of it! You deserve someone whose actions toward you don't require two volumes of apologies and explanations.

Dead Giveaway #2: He's critical

"In retrospect, I didn't even realize how screwed up my relationship was. Of course, it started off great. But very soon—we're talking within weeks—he started pointing out things he didn't

like. He would say I was unreliable if I didn't return his calls within an hour. He would accuse me of being inconsiderate if I was walking too slow, or 'holding up foot traffic,' as he put it. He would even criticize my friends. At the time, I thought he was so smart and gave him way too much credit, so I tried really hard to see things from his point of view. I was so devastated when we finally broke up that it took me over a year to realize what an idiot I'd been and what an insecure little prick he was."
—Laurie, 32, Las Vegas, NV

Destructive criticism simply has no place in a healthy relationship. And by destructive, I don't just mean the old "you're stupid" brand of put-down (which is so obviously out of line that we don't even really need to address it, right?), but any disparaging comment that's either entirely unprovoked or is triggered by something most "normal" people would agree is quite minor.

I had one friend whose fiancé began telling her that he didn't like her body before finally confessing that he was just trying to get out of getting married. Another good friend of mine was married to a guy who consistently treated her with disrespect because he thought that was the only way an underemployed loser like him could keep a pretty, successful girl like her interested. Suffice to say, after she figured this out and divorced him, she had to leave him the house just to avoid paying spousal support.

Whereas love is often blind to most faults, fear and indifference see every flaw. If you're hearing your significant other expressing more and more negativity toward you, avoid these reactions at all costs:

- Trying to change yourself so you can please him.
- Trying to convince him that he's wrong about you.

Instead, muster up every ounce of your strength and courage and walk away with your dignity. Once you're alone, you will have the space and time to think about whether or not he actually had a point when he called you "lazy and irresponsible," or if he was just coming up with arbitrary rationalizations for pushing you away. Either way, you will learn from the experience and move on stronger, wiser, and better suited for a future relationship.

Dead Giveaway #3: He's just not that interested

"I'll never forget that feeling. I loved him so much and he really was a good guy. But he always felt distant. It was clear that he had his thing going on and our relationship was not his priority. I challenged him over and over again to make our relationship his priority, but whenever I brought it up, he just shut down. In the end, I don't know if it was the timing or just me, but I ultimately accepted that he just wasn't that into me when he broke up with me after three-and-a-half years together. I realize now that I've never felt as alone as I did while we were together. I always felt like I was holding on to the relationship for dear life until it just fell to pieces. I'm now single, and after a really tough year, I'm finally excited again about my life and all that I bring to the table."
—Tara, 25, Denver, CO

This story is so common that I'm sure most of you have either felt that way yourselves or have good friends who have walked in Tara's shoes. I'm not going to talk about the signs to look for in order to determine if he's disinterested or taking you for granted. The book *He's Just Not That Into You* did a great job of that already.

Just understand that a relationship can be dysfunctional even if the guy you are dating is wonderful. He may be an absolutely great guy who's just not that into you. He may be brilliant with ten advanced degrees. On paper, he may be everything you want. But if he's not meeting your needs, he's the wrong guy for you. As Tara's story illustrates, just because he's a good guy doesn't mean that you're not going to feel lonely in your relationship. It's how you react to this circumstance that determines everything.

Men Want What They Can't Have

I am going to let you in on a little secret: Men really do want what they can't have. When we invest ourselves in a relationship, we want it to work. However, when you "lose" yourself in the relationship, men quite naturally become scared, or even worse, disinterested. Once a man knows that you've lost yourself to him and he's "got" you, the whole challenge of keeping you is over and his interest is gone. Every time I see it happen I wish I could scream at the top of my lungs: "Don't change for him! Maintain your identity!"

I have a number of girlfriends who have dated guys I know fairly well. These are women who bring a lot to the table. But give them two or three months in the relationship, and everything changes. Take my friend Laura and my good friend Jim. A few years ago I introduced them, thinking they would be perfect together because they were both independent, strong-willed, and self-assured. At least that's what I thought. After two months together, Laura had undergone a complete transformation. She convinced herself that Jim was "the one" and began her slow descent into what can only be called dependency.

She started making all kinds of sacrifices for Jim and then would get angry when he didn't reciprocate. She told him that she loved him and when he didn't say it back, she became extremely defensive. Her carefree nature was gone, and that cool, self-assured girl that Jim had initially met had literally disappeared. I felt torn because they are both great people. Jim confided in me that he really loved Laura, but he loved the Laura he had first met and not the Laura she had become—needy, possessive, and, at times, even vindictive. So Jim walked away, and while I've since patched up my friendship with Laura and she's back to her old self, I can tell she'll always be scarred by that experience.

Here's the point: Sometimes men are assholes in relationships and as a result, women become Lost Girls. Other times, it's just the opposite. Women meet an absolutely incredible guy and become Lost Girls because they focus so hard on holding on to him that they lose sight of themselves. As Lost Girl loses the self-confidence and independence that attracted her boyfriend to her in the first place, he gets scared that she won't be able to survive without him. And rather than bear the enormous weight of that responsibility, he walks away for greener and less stressful pastures.

So, what is the solution? Keep in mind this simple tip: Maintain some of your world for yourself and don't give it *all* to him. Don't give up your hobbies for his hobbies. Don't give up your friends for his friends. Don't ever give away your self-identity. A major reason men get scared in relationships is because we become fearful that you can no longer function without us. And that's too much pressure for anyone to take.

My friend Jon dated a girl for four years and never once told her that he loved her. One day he got up the nerve to break up with her, feeling just terrible and fully expecting her to fall apart. But what did she do? She started dating other guys, ran a few marathons, and otherwise thrived on her own. What did he do? He went begging for her to take him back. It took seeing her succeed on her own for him to realize what a great catch she was. She never lost herself. Score one for the girls! If he knows that you will be fine on your own, he won't be scared, the pressure will be off, and he'll be able to breathe easy and enjoy the relationship. He will also respect you each and every day he is with you.

The Dangers of Becoming a Lost Girl

I know it's not easy to walk away from a relationship. It's even more difficult to walk away from an emotionally abusive relationship, because somewhere along the way you lose your confidence and self-esteem. They don't call it a vicious cycle for nothing. But if you can't leave someone who is emotionally hurtful, what makes you think you'll be able to get out should the abuse turn physical?

If you're thinking, *No way, not me. I would never stand for violence,* keep in mind that this is precisely what most women who have been physically abused thought before getting involved with someone who slowly but surely robbed them of their sense of self to the point where they were willing to put up with anything.

Of course, the situation may never get that aggravated. Maybe you'll just wind up with a broken heart and a bad case of trust issues. But think about the pain that you're tolerating right now, and ask yourself how different it is from the physical pain a battered woman might feel? If you're accepting misery as a natural state of mind, how are you different from the Lost Girl I described earlier in the introduction, the one whose face I had to stitch up, and who inspired me to write this book in the first place?

I wish I could say something that will get you back on the right path today, but if you're an extreme Lost Girl, you're probably addicted to the highs and lows of your bad relationship. In this case, you'll need more than words of encouragement. You'll need to reconnect with your friends, lean on your family, suffer through a host of withdrawal symptoms, and possibly even seek out a professional therapist to help you understand that what your boyfriend put you through isn't right, isn't normal, isn't healthy, and isn't even close to what you deserve out of life.

Date This Guy

Winding up alone is a Lost Girl's greatest fear. Why else would you tolerate someone treating you poorly or ambivalently when you can be treated like a queen or, at the very least, an equal? If you never figure out that being alone is way better than being stuck with a jerk or someone who is indifferent, how are you ever going to get the chance to meet any of these great guys:

- **Mr. Best Friend:** You're so compatible, you wonder if he isn't some fantasy you created in your dreams. You can talk for hours without ever running out of conversation. He supports you and encourages you just like a best friend should.
- **Mr. Considers Your Feelings:** This guy is always putting your needs ahead of his own. He wants to make sure you're happy. Where would you like to eat? What movie would you like to see? He's no pushover, but nothing makes him happier than seeing you happy.
- **Mr. High on Life:** This type of guy has tons of energy and a great zest for life. Being with him is always an adventure. You explore the world together, whether through travel, sports, or a variety of hobbies and activities, and are rarely sitting still.

The point I'm trying to make is that with so many amazing guys out there who can make your life brighter, why are you settling for someone who doesn't even appreciate what you're giving up for him?

It's Not You, It's Him

Nobody is perfect, but if you're with someone who is mistreating you, you are with a person who is so far beneath you that you're pretty near perfect by comparison. I know it's hard to resist the pull of such questions as: *If I'm so great, then why doesn't he love me more?* But please try to understand that in your case, it's not you, it's him. Believe it or not, it may have been some of your best qualities that got you into this situation. For instance, you may never have wound up a Lost Girl if you weren't so:

- **Trusting:** He told you he loved you and you believed him. He told you that he was out with the guys all night and you bought that too. He saw that you trusted him, but instead of respecting that bond, he used your faith against you. Now, you tell me, who is the better person in this scenario?
- **Honest:** Often, it's the most honest people who are the most trusting. It's only natural—you figure that since you wouldn't lie, why would he? Don't beat yourself up for this quality, but do realize that honesty is a value that needs to be shared by both partners if the relationship is to work out.
- **Loyal:** You got into this relationship because you fell in love and decided you wanted to make it work. Just because things are not going as smoothly as you'd hoped doesn't mean you're ready to bail. You're loyal,

and once someone wins your heart, you stand by him through thick and thin. Just make sure the person you're fighting for is worthy of your loyalty.

- **Compassionate:** Your ability to see another person's point of view is truly impressive. You can take your feelings out of the equation and look at any disagreement from both sides. Since relationships are a two-way street, you wouldn't have a problem if your partner was similarly compassionate. You'd both be looking out for each other. Unfortunately, if you're the only one with the compassion gene, you're often trying to understand and help someone who has no interest in doing the same for you. After a while, you may find that your needs are never acknowledged.

Your Rx: Find Yourself

As far as most guys are concerned, nothing is more attractive in a woman than an air of independence. When a guy can see that you're perfectly capable of taking care of yourself, taking control of your own life, and recognizing your own worth, he's much more likely to respect you, seek your affection, and work to keep it. Women who have not found an outlet for their creative and intellectual abilities are much more likely to lose themselves in their relationships. To avoid falling into this trap:

- **Throw yourself into work:** You're the opposite of the Working Girl. While she may not focus on relationships enough, you're now in the process of overdoing it. Yes, you're working on building a future with someone, but like I've been saying, if you allow this to become your solitary pursuit, you're in danger of losing sight of what makes you an individual within the relationship. To combat this possibility, it's time to take your career more seriously—especially if you fall into either of these two categories:

1. **Damsel in Distress:** Why bother? Once we get married, my boyfriend will take me away from all this.
2. **Mother in Waiting:** I'll have to quit to have kids anyway, so what's the point of killing myself to succeed now?

- **Audition new goals and interests:** The next time you have a free moment and find yourself sitting still just staring at your boyfriend or waiting for him to come back from wherever he skipped off to, just get up and do something that interests you. Learn how to surf. Start a garden. Go to the grocery store, buy fresh ingredients, and cook something that you saw on the Food Network. Join a runner's group and start training for a marathon or a 10K.

The idea behind this prescription is to find new, specific goals that aren't related to your relationship so that you can get your mind off your boyfriend and back onto you.

Fake It Till You Make It

Lost Girls may have some trouble getting started on the steps in the Rx section because a lot of them involve figuring out what is important to you—just you and not him. This might be hard if you're spending hours each day trying to appease the irrational complaints of a possessive boyfriend, or working overtime to win the love and respect of an ambivalent guy. That said, here are some steps you can take to get you in the right frame of mind in a hurry:

- **Keep track of your moods:** Sometimes it takes writing things down to make us see the obvious. Keep track of your feelings and moods in a journal to see what types of emotions your boyfriend brings into your life.
- **Remember that talk is cheap:** Forget words and focus on what the two of you are doing. If you're nagging him about his bad behavior one minute and then going out buying him little gifts and treating him to dinner the next, you can't blame him for not changing his ways. And if he's telling you what you want to hear, then going out and doing whatever he pleases, remind yourself that what he says doesn't matter; it's what he does that counts.
- **Watch out for rationalizations:** Stop apologizing and explaining for him. The next time you hear yourself coming to his defense when your friends and family question his behavior, resist the urge to rationalize. Instead, try just as hard to hear their side as you do to understand his.
- **Get out there:** You used to have a life, remember? Now, you're all tangled up in him, but the process of unraveling can begin today. Call up an old friend. Go to lunch with your sister. Make plans for a girls' night out. Remind yourself of how much fun you can have without him.

- **Treat yourself:** Just because your guy isn't giving you what you need doesn't mean you have to give up on yourself. Boost your own ego with a trip to the spa and indulge in a facial or a massage. Start doing what you can to feel good about yourself again.

I realize I have been somewhat discouraging throughout this chapter. I'm sure many of you are saying, "He just doesn't get it—relationships take a lot of work." Yes, relationships *do* take work. So don't go home tonight and tell your loving boyfriend or husband you've had enough and that you're packing your bags. If overall you are content in your relationship, then it is worth fighting for. However, if you cannot honestly say that you are happy in your relationship, you deserve better. Life is too short to be in an unhappy relationship, and it may be time to stop faking it and really make a change. If you are in an unhappy, unsatisfying relationship my ultimate advice is:

- **Walk away:** As hard as this may be to do, if you have become lost in your relationship and are no longer happy, sometimes the only solution is to say good-bye. And while I'm not advocating walking away as a means to any end other than getting away from a bad situation, there is always the chance that after you've left him, he may realize that he is a complete idiot for behaving so poorly. He will quite possibly do everything in his power to get you back. Then, *you* can decide if you're willing to take *him* back.
- **Be willing to hurt:** Walking away and staying away

requires the ability to endure pain and loneliness. Every single bone in your body will urge you to go back to him. Resist the temptation. I promise that over time, the hurt will be replaced with hope and a much more stable state of mind. In the meantime, lean on your trusted family or friends for strength, because you will need it—and they will be only too happy to provide it.

If You Believe in Yourself, He'll Know

I f you are struggling in life or in love, just remember you're not alone. We've all struggled. If you identified with one or more of the women that I outlined in this book, don't beat yourself up. Heck, I'm a man and I've identified with each of those traits at different points in my life. That's only natural. You wouldn't be human if you couldn't relate to any of the girls in the previous chapters. If there's one thing I cannot stress enough, it is this:

At one time or another, *everyone* has been *that* girl.

As you've heard me say before, if something is broken, I want to fix it. Now that we've focused on defining *that* girl, let's stop concentrating on who you don't want to be and start talking about the type of woman you do want to be. There's a reason we all laugh at the guy who is out of work, out of shape, living out of his mom's basement, and thinking that if he wanted he could probably date Jessica Alba. We know that none of us can afford to sit back and do nothing if we ever hope to get what we want out of life.

Whether male or female, we *all* have to slay some dragons and prove ourselves before we can get the girl or guy of our dreams. Except, in real life, those dragons are really just our perceived limitations. You'll recognize them by their proper names, names like "Personal Insecurities," "Lack of Motivation," "Pessimistic Attitude," "Anger at Ex-Boyfriend," and, of course, "Low Self-Esteem." Hopefully, you recognize your own dragons, or limitations, and understand that working to overcome them is going to be a lifelong process.

As you know by now, the goal of this book was to convince you that there is only one person you have to prove yourself to: You. Life is so exhausting if you are constantly trying to impress other people or trying to impress your significant other. Worrying so much about what other people think is what makes a girl *that* girl. It is so much easier if you realize that the only person you need to gain respect from is yourself. Respect from others will follow.

When you become comfortable with yourself, both with the good and the bad, it becomes easier to acknowledge that life is not a competition. Unless you're Tiger Woods or Michael Jordan, you are not likely to be the absolute best at any one thing in your life. Few are equipped with that kind of ability. And that's just fine! In fact, I would argue that it is much more impressive to be a great friend than to be a supermodel on the cover of a fashion magazine. Life is not a competition, so don't feel like you are always measuring yourself against some impossible standard. Be thankful for who you are. Be thankful that you aren't like everyone else. Be thankful for your quirks, because whether you realize it or not, they are what make you such a beautiful, unique person!

Will it always be easy to love yourself and be absolutely confident and comfortable in your own skin? Of course not. It will be a daily challenge. If it were always easy to be supremely

confident, everyone would be good at it! Try to keep it simple.
Simple, as in, you already know what you need to do to feel good
about you. And the more you overanalyze and confuse the issue,
the more likely you are to let your own smoke and mirrors side-
track you from what's really important: your belief in yourself.

Hopefully, this book has demystified what separates *that* girl
from this one: the girl who's got her priorities straight. The girl
who is a good friend. The girl who takes her health seriously. The
girl who has interests that fulfill her. The girl who has something
to say. The girl who has positive energy. In short, the girl who
truly believes in herself.

Will you have your negative, bitter days? Absolutely. Nobody
wakes up every morning feeling bright-eyed and bushy-tailed.
Anyone who pretends otherwise is lying. Just remember, you absolutely do have a choice as to how you approach every day of your
life and your relationships. You *are* in control.

You know as well as I do that people who . . .

- make constant efforts to look on the bright side, even
  in the worst circumstances,
- wake up in the morning feeling good about their
  overall health,
- believe that their jobs and interests are worthwhile,
- have good friends to call when they want to talk,
- fill their free time with activities they enjoy, and
- love and accept themselves for who they are

. . . are happy, confident people!

It makes no difference whether they're single or attached.
Women who are happy and confident don't need to be in a

relationship to be satisfied with themselves and all they have going for them. Balanced, stable, motivated, and dynamic, they've got their acts together and their lives in order. And that's exactly what I want for you. More important, that's what you want for yourself. As long as you are constantly striving to improve yourself and find new avenues for fulfillment in life, then through good times and bad, you'll always end up on the right side of things and happy with yourself.

And that's all any good man really wants—a woman who is happy with herself but always striving to be even better. That is the girl who will eventually find her "Prince Charming." That is the woman any guy would feel lucky to call his own.

About the Authors

Dr. Travis Stork graduated magna cum laude from Duke University and earned his medical degree from the University of Virginia. He currently lives in Colorado where he works as an ER doctor.

Leah Furman has written and co-written twenty-five books, including *Single Jewish Female*, *The Everything Dating Book*, and *Generation Inc.* She lives in New York City.